To:

_____

From:

_____

Date:

_____

To Christiana

Robert J. Morgan is available for speaking engagements
and may be contacted through his Web site at
www.robertjmorgan.com.

Project Editor: Kathy Baker

Design: Jackson Design Co, LLC

ISBN 13: 978-1-4041-0232-3

Printed and bound in the United States of America

www.thomasnelson.com

COME LET US ADORE HIM

STORIES BEHIND THE MOST CHERISHED
CHRISTMAS HYMNS

ROBERT J. MORGAN

THOMAS NELSON
Since 1798

NASHVILLE   DALLAS   MEXICO CITY   RIO DE JANEIRO   BEIJING

Table of Contents

Blessed is the season which engages
the whole world in a conspiracy of love!

HAMILTON WRIGHT MABIE

Prelude

Christmas is a season for singing—a midwinter's epoch of joyful music—and the hymns of Christmas are among the best–known songs in the world. Beginning on that wondrous night when angelic choirs hovered over Bethlehem's fields and down to our own day, Yuletide carols have cheered the world with the greatest news in history. No wonder we sing them from our earliest days to our grayest years.

But not everyone can sing openly this Christmas.

When a group of Korean business leaders recently visited our church, I asked them about the plight of Christians in North Korea. "They have suffered greatly," was the sad reply. "There has been terrible persecution, and thousands of Christians have died for their faith; yet many believers still worship despite danger and death threats. When they gather, it's in complete secrecy; and when they sing, it is done in silence. They open their mouths in unison, but they allow no sound from their voices for fear of being overheard."

The next Sunday, I sang with renewed intensity. It would have been a shame to miss the privilege of lifting my voice to the Lord with all my heart. To paraphrase something Ruth Bell Graham once told me, "We should sing when we feel like it, for it is a shame to miss such an opportunity; we should sing when we don't feel like it, for it is dangerous to remain in such a condition."

Especially at Christmas.

Of our all holy days, it's the Season of the Advent that most invites our songs. In fact, we have a special name for Christmas hymns. We call them *carols*, a word coming from an old Latin word meaning *choral song*.

This volume spans the ages of Christianity, telling the stories of carols ancient and modern. Here you'll find the background of our best–known Christmas hymns, plus a few stories of great carols that have nearly been lost to history.

With this little volume, we invite you: *O Come, Let Us Adore Him!*

Oh, clap your hands, all you peoples!
Shout to God with the voice of triumph!
For the LORD Most High is awesome;
He is a great King over all the earth.
Sing praises to God, sing praises!
Sing praises to our King, sing praises!
For God is the King of all the earth;
Sing praises with understanding.
God reigns over the nations;
God sits on His holy throne.

PSALM 47:1–2, 6–8

From Heaven Above to Earth I Come

1531

Then God blessed them, and God
said to them, "Be fruitful and multiply;
fill the earth and subdue it . . ."

GENESIS 1:28

Martin Luther never expected to marry, for he had taken a vow of celibacy as an Augustinian monk. Even after discovering the great Reformation truths of "Scripture Alone, Faith Alone," he still intended to keep his vow. As the Reformation picked up steam and other monks began to marry, he exclaimed, "Good heavens! They won't give me a wife!"

It wasn't just monks who were renouncing their celibacy, however; it was nuns, too. When Luther heard that a group of nuns from a nearby cloister wanted to escape their situation (which in their case amounted to virtual captivity) he agreed to help them, though doing so was a serious violation of the law. Enlisting the aid of a local merchant named Leonard Kopp, age sixty, Luther arranged for the nuns to be smuggled out in the empty barrels used to deliver herring to the nunnery. It was a fishy plan if ever there was one, but it worked.

Having liberated these women, Luther now felt responsible for placing them in homes. He managed to find husbands for all but one—Katharina Von Bora. Two years passed, and Luther was deeply troubled by his failure to find her a husband. She was now twenty–six years old, brilliant and effervescent, but still unclaimed.

In a visit to his parents, Luther, age forty–two, joked that he might have to marry Katharina himself. His dad heartily endorsed the idea, and the two were married on June 27, 1525.

By autumn, Katharina informed Martin that she was pregnant, and Luther cheerfully announced, "My Katharina is fulfilling Genesis 1:28"— the verse about being fruitful and multiplying.

"There's about to be born a child of a monk and a nun," he bragged to friends. Accordingly, little Hans was born on June 7, 1526.

Luther was devoted to his son, and five years later he wrote this Christmas carol for him. Luther called it "a Christmas child's song concerning the child Jesus," and it was sung each year during the Christmas Eve festivities at Luther's massive home—a former Augustinian monastery—on the upper end of Wittenberg's main street.

For over five hundred years it has been one of Lutheranism's greatest carols, delighting children today just as it thrilled little Hans in the sixteenth century.

The mystery of the humanity of Christ,
that He sunk Himself into our flesh,
is beyond all human understanding.

MARTIN LUTHER

These are fine, heart–warming words—that God
wants to come down to us, God wants to come to
us and we do not need to clamber up to him, he
wants to be with us to the end of the world.

———

MARTIN LUTHER

And the Word became flesh and dwelt among us,
and we beheld His glory, the glory as of the only
begotten of the Father, full of grace and truth.

———

JOHN 1:14

For little children everywhere
A joyous season still we make;
We bring our precious gifts to them,
Even for the dear child Jesus' sake.

———

PHOEBE CARY

From Heaven Above to Earth I Come

Martin Luther, translated by Catherine Windworth

Attr. to Martin Luther

1. From heav'n a - bove to earth I come, to
2. To you, this night, is born a Child Of
3. 'Tis Christ our God, who far on high Had
4. These are the to - kens ye shall mark, The

bear good news to ev - ery home; glad tid - ings of great
Mar - y, chos - en moth - er mild; This ten - der Child of
heard your sad and bit - ter cry; Him - self will your Sal -
swad - dling clothes and man - ger dark; There shall ye find the

joy I bring, Where - of I now will say and sing.
low - ly birth, Shall be the joy of all your earth.
va - tion be, Him - self from sin will make you free.
young Child laid, By Whom the heav'ns and earth were made.

We Sing, Emmanuel, Thy Praise

1654

I will be glad and rejoice in You;
I will sing praise to Your name, O Most High.

PSALM 9:2

Paul Gerhardt might be called the "Charles Wesley of Germany," for he was a prolific hymnist who gave Lutheranism some of its warmest hymns.

Paul grew up in Grafenhaynichen, Germany, where his father was mayor. This village near Wittenberg was devastated by the Thirty Years' War, and Paul's childhood was marked by scenes of bloodshed and death. But he had a good mind and heart, and he enrolled at the University of Wittenberg at age twenty–one.

After graduation, Paul found a job in Berlin tutoring children. During this time, encouraged by Johann Cruger, choirmaster at Berlin's St. Nicholas Church, he began writing hymns. When Cruger published a hymnbook in 1648, Paul was delighted to find his hymns in it. Others were added to later editions. In all, Gerhardt wrote 123 hymns. His hymnody reflects the shift from the rugged theological hymns of Luther to the more subjective, devotional songs of German Pietistic revival. Best known are "Give to the Winds Your Fears," "Jesus, Thy Boundless Love to Me," and "O Sacred Head, Now Wounded" (which he translated).

Paul was ordained into the ministry at age forty–four and began preaching in and around Berlin. In 1651, he became chief pastor at

Mittenwalde, just outside Berlin, and later he returned to Berlin to labor at St. Nicholas Church alongside his mentor, Johann Cruger.

At that point, however, Paul became embroiled in a conflict with the Elector Friedrich Wilhelm, who wanted Lutheran clergymen to sign an edict limiting their freedom of speech on theological matters. Refusing, Paul was deposed from his pulpit in February of 1666. He was even forbidden to lead private worship in his home. During this time, four of his five children died, and in 1668, his wife also passed away.

Late that year, 1668, Paul assumed the pastorate of the Lutheran church in Lubben an der Spree, where he ministered faithfully until his death on May 27, 1676. He was buried in the crypt beneath the altar of the church where he preached. Today the church is known locally as the "Paul Gerhardt Church," and a monument at the entrance reminds visitors of the church's famous pastor–poet.

This Christmas carol, "We Sing, Emmanuel, Thy Praise," has a hauntingly beautiful melody that seems to express the sorrows through which Gerhardt passed. But the words are full of praise, every verse ending in an exuberant "Hallelujah!"

Just like Paul Gerhardt's life.

> God . . . has only one answer to every
> human need—His Son, Jesus Christ.
>
> WATCHMAN NEE

The fact of Jesus' coming is the final and
unanswerable proof that God cares.

WILLIAM BARCLAY

O God, my heart is steadfast;
I will sing and give praise, even with my glory.
Awake, lute and harp! I will awaken the dawn.
I will praise You, O LORD, among the peoples,
And I will sing praises to You among the nations.
For Your mercy is great above the heavens,
And Your truth reaches to the clouds.
Be exalted, O God, above the heavens,
And Your glory above all the earth.

PSALM 108:1–5

Sing praises to the LORD, who dwells in Zion!
Declare His deeds among the people.

PSALM 9:11

We Sing, Emmanuel, Thy Praise

Paul Gerhardt

Nikolaus Hermann

1. We sing, Emmanuel, Thy praise,
2. For Thee, since first the world was made,
3. Now art Thou here, Thou ever blest!
4. But I, Thy servant, Lord, today

Thou Prince of Life and Fount of grace, Thou Flow'r of
So many hearts have watched and prayed; The patri-
In lowly manger dost Thou rest. Thou, making
Confess my love and freely say, I love Thee

heav'n and Star of morn, Thou Lord of
archs' and prophets' throng, For Thee have
all things great, art small; So poor art
truly, but I would That I might

lords, Thou virgin born. Hallelujah!
hoped and waited long. Hallelujah!
Thou, yet clothest all. Hallelujah!
love Thee as I should. Hallelujah!

While Shepherds Watched Their Flocks

1700

He will feed His flock like a shepherd;
He will gather the lambs with His arm,
And carry them in His bosom,
And gently lead those who are with young.

ISAIAH 40:11

This popular carol owes its endurance to two men with dark financial woes.

The first, Naham Tate, was born in Dublin in 1652 to a preacher who was literally named Faithful—Rev. Faithful Teate (original spelling). After attending Trinity College in Dublin, young Naham migrated to London to be a writer. His success was slow in coming, but he dabbled with plays, adapted the prose of others, and eventually was named poet laureate in 1692 and appointed royal historiographer ten years later. Unfortunately, Naham was intemperate and careless in handling money, and he lived in perpetual financial distress. He died in an institution for debtors in 1715.

His chief claim to fame was his collaboration with Nicholas Brady in compiling a hymnbook entitled *The New Version of the Psalms of David*, published in 1696. It was re–issued in 1700 with a supplement in which this carol first appeared. The words to "While Shepherds Watched Their Flocks" represent a very literal paraphrase of Luke 2:8–14, making this one of our most biblically accurate Christmas carols.

The second man instrumental in the song's success was George Frederick Handel, composer of the music to which this carol is sung. Handel was born in Germany with the inborn talent of a musical genius. His father pressured the young man to enter law school, but George would not be denied, writing his first composition by age twelve and amazing choirmasters with his artistry. He eventually moved to London, where he enjoyed great success for a season. Then his popularity waned, his income dwindled, and he went bankrupt. It was the remarkable success of *Messiah* (see page 28) that salvaged Handel's career—and bank account. Through it all, Handel's powerful personality pressed on.

On one occasion, just as a concert was about to begin, his friends gathered to tell him the concert hall was nearly empty. Few people had bought tickets. "Never mind," Handel said after pausing to absorb the news. "The music will sound the better," due to the nearly empty room.

How ironic! These two men never met, they both struggled with poverty, faced bankruptcy, and worried about making ends meet—yet they enriched the world beyond measure, providing millions of people for scores of generations with the gift of song every Advent season.

Shepherds at the grange,
Where the Babe was born,
Sang with many a change,
Christmas carols until morn.

HENRY WADSWORTH LONGFELLOW

The people who walked in darkness
Have seen a great light; Those who dwelt
in the land of the shadow of death,
Upon them a light has shined.

ISAIAH 9:2

Hail the night, and hail the morn,
That beheld the Saviour born!
When in Bethlem's wakeful fold
Tidings good an angel told.

CHARLES L. HUTCHINS

Sing to God, you kingdoms of the
earth; Oh, sing praises to the Lord,
To Him who rides on the heaven of
heavens, which were of old! Indeed,
He sends out His voice, a mighty voice.

PSALM 68:32–33

While Shepherds Watched Their Flocks

Naham Tate

George Friedrich Handel

Joy to the World!

1719

Shout joyfully to the LORD, all the earth;
Break forth in song, rejoice, and sing praises.

PSALM 98:4

Until Isaac Watts came along, most of the singing in British churches was from the Psalms of David. The church—especially the Church of Scotland—had labored over the Psalms with great effort and scholarship, translating them into poems with rhyme and rhythm suitable for singing. As a young man in Southampton, Isaac had become dissatisfied with the quality of singing, and he keenly felt the limitations of being able only to sing the Psalms. So he "invented" the English hymns.

He did not, however, neglect the Psalms. In 1719 he published a unique hymnal—one in which he had translated, interpreted, and paraphrased the Old Testament Psalms through the eyes of New Testament faith. He called it simply *The Psalms of David Imitated in the Language of the New Testament.* Taking various Psalms, he studied them from the perspective of Jesus and the New Testament, and then formed them into verses for singing.

"I have rather expressed myself as I may suppose David would have done if he lived in the days of Christianity," Watts explained, "and by this means, perhaps, I have sometimes hit upon the true intent of the Spirit of God in those verses farther and clearer than David himself could ever discover."

Watt's archrival, Thomas Bradbury, was greatly critical of Watts' songs, which he called *whims* instead of *hymns*. He accused Watts of thinking he was King David. Watts replied in a letter, "You tell me that I rival it with David, the sweet psalmist of Israel. I abhor the thought; while yet, at the same time, I am fully persuaded that the Jewish psalm book was never designed to be the only Psalter for the Christian church."

"Joy to the World!" is Isaac Watts' interpretation of Psalm 98, which says: "Shout joyfully to the LORD, all the earth" (verse 4). As he read Psalm 98, Watts pondered the real reason for shouting forth joyfully to the Lord—the Messiah has come to redeem us. The result, despite the now-forgotten criticisms of men like Bradbury, has been a timeless carol that has brightened our Christmases for nearly three hundred years.

Joy is the serious business of heaven.

C. S. LEWIS

To be a joy–bearer and a joy–giver says everything,
for in our life, if one is joyful, it means that one is
faithfully living for God, and that nothing else
counts; and if one gives joy to others one is doing
God's work; with joy without and joy within,
all is well . . . I can conceive no higher way.

JANET ERSKINE STUART

For unto us a Child is born,
Unto us a Son is given;
And the government will be upon His shoulder.
And His name will be called
Wonderful, Counselor, Mighty God,
Everlasting Father, Prince of Peace.
Of the increase of His government and peace
There will be no end,
Upon the throne of David and over His kingdom,
To order it and establish it with judgment and justice
From that time forward, even forever.

ISAIAH 9:6–7

There is a new wonder in heaven and on earth:
God is on earth and man is in heaven.

THALASSIOS THE LIBYAN

"A woman, when she is in labor, has sorrow
because her hour has come; but as soon as she has
given birth to the child, she no longer remembers
the anguish, for joy that a human being has been
born into the world. Therefore you now have
sorrow; but I will see you again and your heart will
rejoice, and your joy no one will take from you."

JOHN 16:21–22

Joy to the World!

Isaac Watts

George Frederick Handel
Arr. by Lowell Mason

1. Joy to the world! the Lord is come; Let earth re - ceive her
2. Joy to the world! the Sav - ior reigns; Let men their songs em -
3. No more let sin and sor - row grow, Nor thorns in - fest the
4. He rules the world with truth and grace And makes the na - tions

King. Let ev - ery heart pre - pare Him room,
ploy, While fields and floods, Rocks, hills and plains
ground. He comes to make His bless - ings flow
prove The glo - ries of His righ - teous - ness

And heav'n and na - ture sing, And heav'n and na - ture
Re - peat the sound - ing joy, Re - peat the sound - ing
Far as the curse is found, Far as the curse is
And won - ders of His love, And won - ders of His

1. And heav'n and na-ture sing, And

sing, And heav'n, and heav'n and na - ture sing.
joy, Re - peat, re - peat the sound - ing joy.
found, Far as, far as the curse is found.
love, And won - ders, and won - ders of His love.

heav'n and na-ture sing,

Hark! The Herald Angels Sing

1739

Then the angel said to them, "Do not be
afraid, for behold, I bring you good tidings
of great joy which will be to all people."

LUKE 2:10

Upon his conversion, Charles Wesley immediately began writing hymns, each one packed with doctrine, all of them exhibiting strength and sensitivity, both beauty and theological brawn. He wrote constantly, and even on horseback his mind was flooded with new songs. He often stopped at houses along the road and ran in asking for "pen and ink."

He wrote more than six thousand hymns during his life, and he didn't like people tinkering with the words. In one of his hymnals, he wrote: "I beg leave to mention a thought which has been long upon my mind, and which I should long ago have inserted in the public papers, had I not been unwilling to stir up a nest of hornets. Many gentlemen have done my brother and me (though without naming us) the honor to reprint many of our hymns. Now they are perfectly welcome to do so, provided they reprint them just as they are. But I desire they would not attempt to mend them, for they are really not able. None of them is able to mend either the sense or the verse. Therefore, I must beg of them these two favors: either to let them stand just as they are, to take things for better or worse, or to add the true reading in the margin, or at the bottom of the page, that we may no longer be accountable either for the nonsense or the doggerel of other men."

But one man did the church a great favor by polishing one of Charles' best–loved hymns. When Charles was 32, he wrote a Christmas hymn that began:

Hark, how all the welkin rings,
"Glory to the King of kings;
Peace on earth, and mercy mild,
God and sinners reconciled!"
Joyful, all ye nations, rise,
Join the triumph of the skies;
Universal nature say,
"Christ the Lord is born to–day!"

The word "welkin" was an old English term for "the vault of heaven." It was Charles' friend, evangelist George Whitefield, who, when he published this carol in his collection of hymns in 1753, changed the words to the now–beloved, "Hark! The Herald Angels Sing."

Blow, bugles of battle, the marches of peace;
East, west, north, and south let the long quarrel cease;
Sing the song of great joy that the angels began,
Sing the glory to God and of good–will to man!

JOHN GREENLEAF WHITTIER

Christmas Day declares that He dwelt among us . . .
it binds together the life of Christ on earth with
His life in heaven; it assures us that Christmas
Day belongs not to time but to eternity.

FREDERICK DENISON MAURICE

"When the Son of Man comes in His glory,
and all the holy angels with Him, then
He will sit on the throne of His glory."

MATTHEW 25:31

"Remember the former things of old,
For I am God, and there is no other;
I am God, and there is none like Me,
Declaring the end from the beginning,
And from ancient times things that are not yet done,
Saying, 'My counsel shall stand,
And I will do all My pleasure,' . . .
Indeed I have spoken it; I will also bring it to pass.
I have purposed it; I will also do it. . . .
I bring My righteousness near, it shall not be far off;
My salvation shall not linger.
And I will place salvation in Zion,
For Israel My glory."

ISAIAH 46:9–11, 13

Hark! The Herald Angels Sing

Charles Wesley   Felix Mendelssohn

1. Hark! the her - ald an - gels sing, "Glo - ry to the new - born King;
2. Christ, by high - est heav'n a - dored, Christ, the ev - er - last - ing Lord;
3. Hail the heav'n born Prince of Peace! Hail the Sun of Righ-teous-ness!

Peace on earth and mer - cy mild, God and sin - ners rec - on - ciled."
Late in time be - hold Him come, Off - spring of a vir-gin's womb.
Light and life to all He brings, Ris'n with heal - ing in His wings.

Joy - ful, all ye na - tions, rise, Join the tri - umph of the skies;
Veiled in flesh the God - head see, Hail, th'in - car - nate De - i - ty!
Mild He lays His glo - ry by, Born that man no more may die;

With an - gel - ic hosts pro-claim, "Christ is born in Beth - le - hem."
Pleased as man with men to dwell, Je - sus our Em - man - u - el.
Born to raise the sons of earth, Born to give them sec - ond birth.

Hallelujah Chorus
(from *The Messiah*)
1741

Let the heavens rejoice, and let the earth be glad;
and let them say among the nations, "The LORD reigns."

---

1 CHRONICLES 16:31

His father tried to discourage his musical interests, preferring that he enter the legal profession. But the organ, harpsichord, and violin captured the heart of young George Frideric Handel. Once, accompanying his father to the court of Duke Johann Adolf, George wandered into the chapel, found the organ, and started improvising. The startled Duke exclaimed, "Who is this remarkable child?"

This "remarkable child" soon began composing operas, first in Italy, then in London. By his twenties, he was the talk of England and the best-paid composer on earth. He opened the Royal Academy of Music. Londoners fought for seats at his every performance, and his fame soared around the world.

But the glory passed. Audiences dwindled. His music became outdated, and he was thought of as an old fogey. Newer artists eclipsed the aging composer. One project after another failed, and Handel, now bankrupt, grew depressed. The stress brought on a case of palsy that crippled some of his fingers. "Handel's great days are over," wrote Frederick the Great, "his inspiration is exhausted."

Yet his troubles also matured him, softening his sharp tongue. His temper mellowed, and his music became more heartfelt. One morning Handel received by post a manuscript from Charles Jennens. It was a word–for–word collection of biblical texts about Christ. The opening words from Isaiah 40 moved Handel: *Comfort ye, comfort ye my people.* . . .

On August 22, 1741, Handel shut the door of his London home and started composing music for the words. Twenty–three days later, the world had *Messiah*. "Whether I was in the body or out of the body when I wrote it, I know not," Handel later said, trying to describe the experience. *Messiah* opened in London to enormous crowds on March 23, 1743, with Handel leading from his harpsichord. King George II, who was present that night, surprised everyone by leaping to his feet during the "Hallelujah Chorus." No one knows why. Some believe the king, being hard of hearing, thought it the national anthem.

No matter—from that day audiences everywhere have stood in reverence during the stirring words: *Hallejulah! For He shall reign forever and ever.*

Handel's fame was rekindled, and even after he lost his eyesight, he continued playing the organ for performances of his oratorios until his death in London, April 14, 1759.

Hail to the King of Bethlehem,
Who weareth in his diadem
The yellow crocus for the gem
Of his authority!

HENRY WADSWORTH LONGFELLOW

And I heard, as it were, the voice of a great
multitude, as the sound of many waters and as the
sound of mighty thunderings, saying, "Alleluia!
For the Lord God Omnipotent reigns!"

REVELATION 19:6

This is the month, and this the happy morn,
Wherein the Son of Heaven's eternal King,
Of wedded maid and virgin mother born,
Our great redemption from above did bring,
For so the holy sages once did sing,
That He our deadly forfeit should release,
And with His Father work us a perpetual peace.

JOHN MILTON

"The glory of the LORD shall be revealed,
And all flesh shall see it together;
For the mouth of the LORD has spoken."

ISAIAH 40:5

Hallelujah Chorus

from *The Messiah*

George Frideric Handel

George Frideric Handel

Hal - le - lu-jah! Hal - le - lu-jah! Hal - le - lu-jah! Hal-le-lu-jah! Hal-

le - lu-jah! Hal - le - lu-jah! Hal - le - lu-jah! Hal-le-

lu-jah! Hal-le - lu-jah! Hal - le - lu-jah! For the Lord

God om-nip - o-tent reign-eth. Hal - le - lu-jah!

O Come, All Ye Faithful
1743

And when they had come into the house, they saw
the young Child with Mary His mother, and fell
down and worshiped Him. And when they had
opened their treasures, they presented gifts to
Him: gold, frankincense, and myrrh.

MATTHEW 2:11

John Francis Wade, author of this hymn, was hounded out of England. He was a Roman Catholic layman in Lancashire; but because of persecution arising from the Jacobite rebellion, streams of Catholics fled to France and Portugal, where communities of English—speaking Catholics appeared.

But how could he, a refugee, support himself? In those days, the printing of musical scores was cumbersome, and copying them by hand was an art. In the famous Roman Catholic College and Ministry Center in Douay, France, Wade taught music and became renowned as a copyist of musical scores. His work was exquisite.

In 1743, Wade, 32, had produced a Latin Christmas carol beginning with the phrase *Adeste Fidelis, Laeti triumphantes*. At one time historians believed he had simply discovered an ancient hymn by an unknown author, but most scholars now believe Wade himself composed the lyrics. Seven original hand–copied manuscripts of this Latin hymn have been found, all of them bearing Wade's signature.

John Wade passed away on August 16, 1786, at age 75. His obituary honored him for his "beautiful manuscripts" that adorned chapels and homes.

As time passed, English Catholics began returning to Britain, and they carried Wade's Christmas carol with them. One day an Anglican minister named Rev. Frederick Oakeley, who preached at Margaret Street Chapel in London, came across Wade's Latin Christmas carol. Deeply moved, he translated it into English for Margaret Street Chapel. The first line of Oakeley's translation said: "Ye Faithful, Approach Ye."

Somehow, "Ye Faithful, Approach Ye," didn't catch on, and several years later Oakeley tried again. By this time, Oakeley, too, was a Roman Catholic priest, having converted to Catholocism in 1845. Perhaps his grasp of Latin had improved, because as he repeated over and over the Latin phrase *Adeste Fidelis, Laeti triumphantes* he finally came up with the simpler, more vigorous *O Come, All Ye Faithful, Joyful and Triumphant!*

So two brave Englishmen, Catholics, lovers of Christmas and lovers of hymns, living a hundred years apart, writing in two different nations, combined their talents to bid us come, joyful and triumphant, and adore Him born the King of angels.

We consider Christmas as the encounter, the great
encounter, the historical encounter, the decisive
encounter, between God and mankind. He who
has faith knows this truly; let him rejoice.

POPE PAUL VI

Without faith it is impossible to please Him, for he
who comes to God must believe that He is, and that
He is a rewarder of those who diligently seek Him.

HEBREWS 11:6

Our Lord says to every living soul,
"I became man for you. If you do not
become God for Me, you do Me wrong."

MEISTER ECKHART

And I heard a loud voice from heaven saying,
"Behold, the tabernacle of God is with men,
and He will dwell with them, and they shall be
His people. God Himself will be with them and be
their God. And God will wipe away every tear from
their eyes; there shall be no more death, nor
sorrow, nor crying. There shall be no more pain,
for the former things have passed away."

REVELATION 21:3–4

O Come, All Ye Faithful

ascribed to John Francis Wade
translated by Frederick Oakeley

John Francis Wade

1. O come all ye faith - ful, Joy - ful and tri - um - phant, O
2. Sing choirs of an - gels, Sing in ex - ul - ta - tion, O
3. Yea, Lord, we greet Thee, Born this hap - py morn - ing;

come ye, O come ye to Beth - le - hem. Come and be -
sing all ye bright Hosts of heav'n a - bove. Glo - ry to
Je - sus to Thee be all glo - ry giv'n. Word of the

hold Him, Born the King of an - gels.
God, All glo - ry in the high - est.
Fa - ther Now in flesh ap - pear - ing.

Refrain

O come let us a - dore Him, O

come let us a - dore Him, O come let us a - dore Him, Christ the Lord.

Come, Thou Long Expected Jesus
1744

You therefore must endure hardship
as a good soldier of Jesus Christ.

2 TIMOTHY 2:3

It's hard to imagine the difficulties faced by John and Charles Wesley and their fellow evangelists as they traveled by horseback from town to town, facing mobs, enduring harsh conditions and severe weather. Here is a sampling from Charles' journal as he pressed into Wales in March of 1748.

Wed., March 23rd. I was . . . not to set out till past seven. The continual rain and sharp wind were full in my teeth. I rode all day in great misery, and had a restless, painful night at Tan–y–bwlch.

Thur., March 24th. I resolved to push for Garth, finding my strength would never hold out for three more days riding. At five (a.m.), I set out in hard rain, which consumed all day. We went through perils of water. I was quite gone when we came at night to a little village. There was no fire in the poor hut. A brother supplied us with some, nailed up our window, and helped us to bed. I had no more rest than the night before.

Fri., March 25th. I took horse again at five, the rain attending us still. . . . The weather was more severe. The violent wind drove the hard rain full in our faces. I rode till I could ride no more; walked the last hour; and by five dropped down at Garth.

Charles' primary purpose in going to Garth was to preach, but he had another motive as well. It was also to see Miss Sally Gwynee, whom he wanted to marry. Marriage required a regular income, however, and Sally's parents were concerned about Charles' ability to sustain a family with no regular source of finances. Charles agreed to publish two volumes of his *Hymns and Sacred Poems.*

The income from royalties more than satisfied Sally's parents, and the two were married on Saturday, April 8, 1749.

"Come, Thou Long–Expected Jesus" wasn't introduced in this two–volume set of *Hymns and Sacred Songs* containing a total of 455 hymns. It had been published earlier, in a 1745 edition of Christmas hymns entitled *Hymns for the Nativity of Our Lord.* This little hymnal contained eighteen Christmas carols Charles had written, of which "Come, Thou Long–Expected Jesus" is the best known.

Oh thou who camest from above
The pure celestial fire to impart,
Kindle a flame of sacred love
On the mean altar of my heart.

CHARLES WESLEY

"From [David's] seed, according to the promise,
God raised up for Israel a Savior—Jesus."

ACTS 13:23

And He was handed the book of the prophet
Isaiah. And when He had opened the book,
He found the place where it was written:
"The Spirit of the LORD is upon Me,
Because He has anointed Me
To preach the gospel to the poor;
He has sent Me to heal the brokenhearted,
To proclaim liberty to the captives
And recovery of sight to the blind,
To set at liberty those who are oppressed;
To proclaim the acceptable year of the LORD."
Then He closed the book, and gave it back to the
attendant and sat down. And the eyes of all who
were in the synagogue were fixed on Him. And He
began to say to them, "Today this Scripture
is fulfilled in your hearing."

LUKE 4:17–21

God is in our midst; He is now here. In Him we live
and move and have our being. Our very bodies
become His temples, and our lives must daily be
fashioned after the pattern of His presence.

J. C. MASSEE

Come, Thou Long-Expected Jesus

Charles Wesley

Rowland H. Prichard

1. Come, Thou long ex-pect-ed Je-sus,
From our fears and sins re-lease us,
2. Born Thy peo-ple to de-liv-er,
Born to reign in us for-ev-er,

Born to set Thy peo-ple free;
Let us find our rest in Thee.
Born a Child and yet a King;
Now Thy gra-cious king-dom bring.

Is-rael's strength and con-so-la-tion, Hope of all the
By Thine own e-ter-nal Spir-it, Rule in all our

earth Thou art; Dear de-sire of ev-ery
hearts a-lone; By Thine all-suf-fi-cient

na-tion, Joy of ev-ery long-ing heart.
mer-it, Raise us to Thy glo-rious throne.

Angels, from the Realms of Glory
1816

Praise Him, all His angels;
Praise Him, all His hosts!

***

PSALM 148:2

Like all Moravians, John Montgomery had a burden for world evangelism. He was the only Moravian pastor in Scotland, but he and his wife felt God's call to be missionaries to the island of Barbados. Tearfully placing their six–year–old son, James, in a Moravian settlement near Ballymena, County Antrim, Ireland, they sailed away. James never saw them again, for they perished in Barbados.

Left with nothing, James was enrolled in a school in England. When he didn't do well, he was apprenticed by school authorities to a baker. Baking wasn't for James. He ran away and spent his teenage years drifting from pillar to post, writing poetry, and trying his hand at one thing then another. He eventually settled down in Sheffield, England.

In his early twenties, James began working for the local newspaper, the *Sheffield Register*, and there he found his niche. He loved writing. It was a politically active newspaper, and when its owner suddenly had to flee the country to avoid persecution and imprisonment, James purchased the paper and renamed it the *Sheffield Iris*. His editorials, too, proved unpopular with local officials. On two separate occasions he was thrown into jail. But he emerged from prison a celebrity, and he used his newly acquired fame to promote his favorite issues.

Chief among his interests was the gospel. Despite the loss of his parents, James Montgomery remained devoted to Christ and to the Scriptures, and he championed the cause of foreign missions and of the British Bible Society.

As the years passed, he became the most respected leader in Sheffield, and its citizens eagerly read his writings. Early on Christmas Eve, 1816, James, 45, opened his Bible to Luke 2 and was deeply impressed by verse 13. Pondering the story of the heralding angels, he took his pen and started writing. By the end of the day, his new Christmas poem was being read in the pages of his newspaper. It was later set to music and was first sung on Christmas Day, 1821, in a Moravian Church in England: "Angels, from the Realms of Glory."

His parents would have been proud.

Ring out ye crystal spheres!
Once bless our human ears,
If ye have power to touch our senses so;
And let your silver chime
Move in melodious time,
And let the bass of Heaven's deep organ blow;
And with your ninefold harmony
Make up full consort to the angelic symphony.

JOHN MILTON

Bless the LORD, you His angels,
Who excel in strength, who do His word,
Heeding the voice of His word.
Bless the LORD, all you His hosts,
You ministers of His, who do His pleasure.
Bless the LORD, all His works,
In all places of His dominion.
Bless the LORD, O my soul!

PSALM 103:20–22

Music is well said to be the speech of
angels; in fact, nothing among the
utterances allowed to man is felt to be
so divine. It brings us near to the infinite.

THOMAS CARLYLE

"Likewise, I say to you, there is joy in the presence
of the angels of God over one sinner who repents."

LUKE 15:10

Angels, from the Realms of Glory

James Montgomery

Henry T. Smart

1. An - gels from the realms of glo - ry, Wing your flight o'er
2. Shep - herds in the fields a - bi - ding, Watch - ing o'er your
3. Sag - es, leave your con - tem - pla - tions, Bright - er vi - sions
4. Saints, be - fore the al - tar bend - ing, Watch - ing long in
5. All cre - a - tion, join in prais - ing, God, the Fath - er,

all the earth; Ye who sang cre - a - tion's sto - ry,
flocks by night; God with man is now re - sid - ing,
beam a - far; Seek the great De - sire of na - tions,
hope and fear; Sud - den - ly the Lord, de - scend - ing,
Spir - it, Son; Ev - er - more your voic - es rais - ing,

Now pro - claim Mes - si - ah's birth.
Yon - der shines the in - fant Light.
Ye have seen His na - tal star.
In His tem - ple shall ap - pear.
To th'et - er - nal Three in One.

Come and wor - ship, come and wor - ship; Wor - ship Christ, the new - born King!

Silent Night
1818

"Therefore the Lord Himself will give you a
sign: Behold, the virgin shall conceive and
bear a Son, and shall call His name Immanuel."

ISAIAH 7:14

It was Christmas Eve in the Austrian Alps. At the newly constructed Church of St. Nicholas in Oberndorf, a Tyrol village near Salzburg, Father Joseph Mohr prepared for the midnight service. He was distraught because the church organ was broken, ruining prospects for that evening's carefully planned music. But Father Joseph was about to learn that our problems are God's opportunities, that the Lord causes all things to work together for good to those who love Him. It came into Father Joseph's mind to write a new song, one that could be sung without the organ. Hastily, he wrote the words, "Silent night, holy night, all is calm, all is bright . . ." Taking the text to his organist, Franz Gruber, he explained the situation and asked Franz to compose a simple tune.

That night, December 24, 1818, "Silent Night" was sung for the first time as a duet accompanied by a guitar at the aptly named Church of St. Nicholas in Oberndorf.

Shortly afterward, as Karl Mauracher came to repair the organ, he heard about the near–disaster on Christmas Eve. Acquiring a copy of the text and tune, he spread the hymn throughout the Alpine region of Austria, referring to it as "Tiroler Volkslied."

The song came to the attention of the Strasser family, makers of fine chamois–skin gloves. To drum up business at various fairs and festivals, the four Strasser children would sing in front of their parents' booth. Like the Von Trapp children a century later, they became popular folk singers throughout the Alps.

When the children—Caroline, Joseph, Andreas, and Amalie—began singing "Trioler Volkslied" at their performances, audiences were charmed. It seemed perfect for the snow–clad region and perfect for the Christian heart. "Silent Night" even came to the attention of the king and queen, and the Strasser children were asked to give a royal performance, assuring the carol's fame.

"Silent Night" was first published for congregational singing in 1838 in the German hymnbook *Katholisches Gesang—und Gebetbuch fur den offentlichen and hauslichen Gottesdienst zunachst zum Gebrauche der katholischen Gereinden im Konigreiche Sachsen*. It was used in America by German–speaking congregations, then appeared in its current English form in a book of Sunday school songs in 1863.

Were it not for a broken organ, there never would have been a "Silent Night."

As fits the holy Christmas birth,
Be this, good friends, our carol still—
Be peace on earth, be peace on earth,
To men of gentle will.

WILLIAM MAKEPEACE THACKERAY

"The Holy Spirit will come upon you, and
the power of the Highest will overshadow
you; therefore, also, that Holy One who is
to be born will be called the Son of God. . . .
For with God nothing will be impossible."

LUKE 1:35, 37

The time draws near the birth of Christ:
The moon is hid; the night is still;
The Christmas bells from hill to hill
Answer each other in the mist.

ALFRED, LORD TENNYSON

Let the peace of God rule in your
hearts, to which also you were called
in one body; and be thankful.

COLOSSIANS 3:15

Silent Night

Joseph Mohr

Franz Gruber

1. Si - lent night, ho - ly night, All is calm, all is bright. Round yon vir - gin moth - er and child; Ho - ly in - fant, so ten - der and mild, Sleep in heav - en - ly peace; Sleep in heav - en - ly peace.

2. Si - lent night, ho - ly night, Shep - herds quake at the sight. Glo - ries stream from heav - en a - far, Heaven - ly hosts sing "Al - le - lu - ia. Christ the Sa - vior is born; Christ the Sav - ior is born."

3. Si - lent night, ho - ly night, Won - drous star, lend thy light. With the an - gels, let us sing, Al - le - lu - ia to our King. Christ the Sa - vior is born; Christ the Sa - vior is born.

4. Si - lent night, ho - ly night, Son of God, love's pure light. Ra - diant beams from Thy ho - ly face, With the dawn of re - deem - ing grace. Je - sus, Lord, at Thy birth; Je - sus, Lord, at Thy birth.

The First Noel

1823

Now there were in the same country
shepherds living out in the fields,
keeping watch over their flock by night.

―――――

LUKE 2:8

No other carol inspires such a mood. The sweet, plaintive strains of "The First Noel," quietly sung on a snow–clad Christmas Eve, bring tears to the eyes and gentle peace to the heart. *Noel, noel, noel, noel. Born is the King of Israel.*

If only we knew who wrote it! It first appeared anonymously in *Some Ancient Christmas Carols*, published by David Gilbert in 1823, and the traditional music evidently came from an unknown source in the west of England.

The poetry itself is plain. If we were to recite this rather lengthy piece, we'd get only a garbled sense of the Christmas story. There's no indication in Scripture, for example, that the shepherds saw the Magi's star. And the final verse of the original carol seems anticlimactic, but when combined with its wistful music, the words glow and our hearts are strangely warmed.

The word "Noel" seems to be a French word with Latin roots: *Natalis,* meaning *birthday.*

Modern hymns omit several of the verses. Here are the last four:

This star drew nigh to the northwest; o'er Bethlehem it took its rest.
And there it did both stop and stay, right over the place where Jesus lay.

Then they did know assuredly within that house, the King did lie
One entered in then for to see and found the babe in poverty.

Then entered in those wise men three, full reverently, upon bended knee,
And offered there, in His presence, their gold and myrrh and frankincense.

If we in our time do well we shall be free from death and hell
For God hath prepared for us all a resting place in general.

Noel, Noel, Noel, Noel; Born is the King of Israel.

Christians awake, salute the happy morn
Whereon the Savior of the world was born.

JOHN BYROM

O Zion,
You who bring good tidings,
Get up into the high mountain;
O Jerusalem,
You who bring good tidings,
Lift up your voice with strength,
Lift it up, be not afraid;
Say to the cities of Judah,
"Behold your God!"

ISAIAH 40:9

Music, the greatest good that mortals know,
And all of heaven we have below.

JOSEPH ADDISON

"I see Him, but not now;
I behold Him, but not near;
A Star shall come out of Jacob;
A Scepter shall rise out of Israel,
And batter the brow of Moab,
And destroy all the sons of tumult."

NUMBERS 24:17

The First Noel

Traditional English Carol

Traditional English Melody

1. The first No - el, the an - gel did say, Was to cer - tain poor
2. They look - ed up and saw a star Shin-ing in the
3. And by the light of that same star, Three Wise Men
4. Then en - tered in those Wise Men three, Full rev - erent-

shep-herds, in fields as they lay; In fields where they lay
east, be - yond them far, And to the earth it
came from coun - try far; To seek for a King was
ly up - on their knee, And of - fered there, in

keep-ing their sheep, On a cold win-ter's night that was so deep.
gave great light, And so it con - tin - ued both day and night.
their in - tent, And to fol - low the star, wher - ev - er it went.
His pres - ence, Their gold, and myrrh, and frank - in - cense.

No - el, No - el, No - el, No - el, Born is the King of Is - ra - el.

O Holy Night
1847

... The star which they had seen in the
East went before them, till it came and
stood over where the young Child was.

MATTHEW 2:9

The words of "O Holy Night" were written in 1847 by a French wine merchant named Placide Clappeau, the mayor of Roquemaure, a town in the south of France. We know little about him except that he wrote poems as a hobby.

We know more about the man who composed the music, a Parisian named Adolphe Charles Adam. The son of a concert pianist, Adams was trained almost from infancy in music and piano. In his mid–twenties, he wrote his first opera and thereafter wrote two operas a year until his death at age fifty–two. Near the end of his life, he lost his savings in a failed business venture involving the French national opera, but the Paris Conservatory rescued him by appointing him professor of music.

It was John Dwight, son of Yale's president, Timothy Dwight ("I Love Thy Kingdom, Lord") who discovered this French carol, "Christian Midnight," and translated it into the English hymn "O Holy Night."

After graduating from Harvard and Cambridge, John Dwight was ordained as minister of the Unitarian church in Northampton, but his pastoring experience wasn't happy. In 1841, George and Sophia Ripley founded a commune named Brook Farm "to prepare a society of liberal, intelligent, and cultivated persons, whose relations with each other would permit a more simple and wholesome life." John was hired as director of the Brook Farm School and began writing a regular column on music for the commune's publication.

Greatly influenced by the liberal views of Ralph Waldo Emerson, he became fascinated by the German culture, especially the symphonic music of Ludwig van Beethoven, and it was largely his influence that introduced Americans to Beethoven's genius.

When Brook Farm collapsed in 1847, John Dwight moved into a cooperative house in Boston and established a career in music journalism. He penned articles on music for major publications, and in 1852 he launched his own publication, *Dwight's Journal of Music*. He became America's first influential classical music critic. He was opinionated, sometimes difficult, a great promoter of European classical music, and an early advocate of Transcendentalism.

How odd that a wine merchant, a penniless Parisian, and a liberal clergyman should give Christianity one of its holiest hymns about the birth of Jesus Christ, Savior of the world.

Great little One! whose all–embracing birth
Lifts Earth to Heaven, stoops Heaven to Earth.

RICHARD CRASHAW

But when the fullness of the time had come, God
sent forth His Son, born of a woman, born under
the law, to redeem those who were under the law,
that we might receive the adoption as sons.

GALATIANS 4:4–5

Fail not to call to mind, in the course of the
twenty–fifth of this month, that the Divinest Heart
that ever walked the earth was born on that day;
and then smile and enjoy yourselves for the
rest of it; for mirth is also of Heaven's making.

LEIGH HUNT

The angel said to her, "Do not be afraid, Mary, for
you have found favor with God. And behold, you
will conceive in your womb and bring forth a Son,
and shall call His name Jesus. He will be great, and
will be called the Son of the Highest; and the Lord
God will give Him the throne of His father David.
And He will reign over the house of Jacob forever,
and of His kingdom there will be no end."

LUKE 1:30–33

O Holy Night

Placide Clappeau

Adolphe Charles Adam

Fall on your knees! O hear the an - gel voic - es! O night di - vine! O night when Christ was born, O night di - vine! O night, O night di - vine!

Once in Royal David's City
1848

Joseph also went up from Galilee, out of the city of
Nazareth, into Judea, to the city of David, which is
called Bethlehem, because he was of the house and
lineage of David, to be registered with Mary, his
betrothed wife, who was with child.

LUKE 2:4–5

Cecil Frances Humphreys was born in 1818, in a tiny Irish village called
Redcross. Thirty–two years later, she married Rev. William Alexander,
and the couple became a powerful duo in British Christianity. William
was appointed the Bishop for all Ireland, but his wife's fame eclipsed his
own. Her poems and hymns became greatly beloved throughout the
English-speaking world.

Mrs. Alexander had a deep heart for children, devoting much time to
teaching Sunday school and writing songs for youngsters. She helped
established a school for the deaf and founded a Girl's Friendly Society in
Londonderry. She worked tirelessly to provide food for the hungry and
comfort to the sick.

One day, Mrs. Alexander was working with one of her Sunday school
pupils—a little boy who happened to be her godson. He was struggling
to understand the Apostle's Creed and certain portions of the Catechism.
Mrs. Alexander began to mull the possibility of converting the Apostles'
Creed into songs for children, using simple little hymns to explain the

phrases and truths of the Christian faith to little ones.

The Apostles' Creed begins: *I believe in God, the Father Almighty, Maker of heaven and earth, and in Jesus Christ, His only Son, our Lord.* For the phase, "Maker of heaven and earth . . ." the creative teacher wrote the famous song "All Things Bright and Beautiful."

The Creed goes on to say about Jesus Christ: *. . . who was conceived of the Holy Spirit, born of the Virgin Mary.* . . . That spurred the writing of the great Christmas carol "Once in Royal David's City."

The next phrase, *suffered under Pontius Pilate, was crucified, died, and was buried,* became the basis for the hymn "There is a Green Hill Far Away."

The Creed goes on to speak of the Second Coming of Christ, prompting Mrs. Alexander to write a lesser-known, beautiful hymn entitled "He is Coming! He is Coming!" which contrasts the Lord's first coming as a babe with His return in power and glory.

These hymns were published in 1848 in Mrs. Alexander's book, *Hymns for Little Children.* It became one of the most successful hymn publishing projects in history, going through more than one hundred editions and telling children the world over what happened "once in royal David's city."

And so the Word had flesh and wrought
With human hands and the creed of creeds,
In loveliness of perfect deeds
More strong than all poetic thought.

ALFRED, LORD TENNYSON

Then let every heart
keep Christmas within.
Christ's pity for sorrow,
Christ's hatred for sin,
Christ's care for the weakest,
Christ's courage for right.
Everywhere, everywhere,
Christmas tonight!

PHILLIPS BROOKS

"... Let me speak freely to you of the patriarch
David, ... knowing that God had sworn with an
oath to him that of the fruit of his body, according
to the flesh, He would raise up the Christ to sit on
his throne, he, foreseeing this, spoke concerning
the resurrection of the Christ ... This Jesus God
has raised up, of which we are all witnesses."

ACTS 2:29–32

Once In Royal David's City

Nahum Tate

George Friedrich Handel

1. Once in roy - al Da - vid's cit - y Stood a low - ly cat - tle shed, Where a moth - er laid her Ba - by In a man - ger for His bed: Mar - y was that moth - er mild, Je - sus Christ her lit - tle Child.

2. He came down to earth from Heav - en, Who is God and Lord of all, And His shel - ter was a sta - ble, And His cra - dle was a stall; With the poor, and mean, and low - ly, Lived on earth our Sav - ior ho - ly.

3. For He is our child - hood's pat - tern; Day by day, like us He grew; He was lit - tle, weak, and help - less, Tears and smiles like us He knew; And He feel - eth for our sad - ness, And He shar - eth in our glad - ness.

4. And our eyes at last shall see Him, Through His own re - deem - ing love, For that Child so dear and gen - tle Is our Lord in Heav'n a - bove, And He leads His chil - dren on To the place where He is gone.

It Came Upon a Midnight Clear
1848

And behold, an angel of the Lord stood before
them, and the glory of the Lord shone
around them, and they were greatly afraid.

LUKE 2:9

Edmund Hamilton Sears is the author of two Christmas carols that are
mirror images of each other, written fifteen years apart.

He was born in Sandisfield, Massachusetts, on April 6, 1819, and
attended Union College in Schenectady, then Harvard Divinity School. He
was ordained in the Unitarian ministry and chose to devote himself to small
towns in Massachusetts, where he had time to study, think, and write.

At 24, he wrote "Calm on the Listening Ear," a carol based on the
song of the angels in Luke 2. It can be sung to the same tune as the
more–famous carol he would later write:

> *Calm on the listening ear of night*
> *Come heaven's melodious strains,*
> *Where wild Judea stretches far*
> *Her silver–mantled plains.*
> *Celestial choirs, from courts above,*
> *Shed sacred glories there,*
> *And angels, with their sparkling lyres,*
> *Make music on the air.*

Fifteen years later, he wrote its famous twin. "It Came Upon the Midnight Clear" is an unusual carol that there is no mention of Christ, of the newborn Babe, or of the Savior's Mission. Sears, after all, was Unitarian. The author's only focus is the angelic request for peace on earth.

Notice again the date of the hymn. It was written as the clouds of civil strife were darkening the United States, setting the stage for the War Between the States. We can grasp the concern that drove Edmund to write this hymn by reading a stanza now usually omitted from most hymnals:

Yet with the woes of sin and strife
The world hath suffered long;
Beneath the angel-strain have rolled
Two thousand years of wrong;
And man, at war with man, hears not
The love song which they bring;
O hush the noise, ye men of strife,
And hear the angels sing!

Edmund Sears became well-known because of his hymns and books. He was awarded a Doctor of Divinity degree in 1871 and took a preaching tour of England, where he was met by large congregations. He died in Weston, Massachusetts, on January 16, 1876.

The angel of the LORD encamps
all around those who fear Him,
And delivers them.

PSALM 34:7

The earth has grown old with its burden of care
But at Christmas it always is young,
The heart of the jewel burns lustrous and fair
And its soul full of music breaks the air,
When the song of angels is sung.

PHILLIPS BROOKS

For He Himself is our peace, who has made
both one, and has broken down the middle
wall of separation . . . And He came and
preached peace to you who were afar off
and to those who were near. For through Him
we both have access by one Spirit to the Father.

EPHESIANS 2:14, 17–18

It Came upon the Midnight Clear

Edmund H. Sears

Richard Storrs Willis

1. It came up-on the mid-night clear, That glo-rious song of old;
2. Still thro' the clo-ven skies they come, With peace-ful wings un-furled;
3. For lo, the days are has-tening on, By proph-et bards fore-told;

From an-gels bend-ing near the earth To touch their harps of gold.
And still their heaven-ly mu-sic floats, O'er all the wear-y world.
When with the ev-er-cir-cling years, Comes round the age of gold.

"Peace on the earth good will to men, From heaven's all gra-cious King!"
A-bove its sad and low-ly plains, They bend on hov-ering wing;
When peace shall o-ver all the earth, Its an-cient splen-dors fling;

The world in sol-emn still-ness lay To hear the an-gels sing.
And ev-er o'er its Ba-bel sounds The bless-ed an-gels sing.
And the whole world give back the song Which now the an-gels sing.

O Come, O Come Emmanuel
1851

"Behold, the virgin shall be with child, and
bear a Son, and they shall call His name
Immanuel," which is translated "God with us."

The origins of this plaintive carol date to medieval times. In the 800s,
a series of Latin hymns were sung each day during Christmas
Vespers from December 17 to 23. Each of these hymns began with the
word "O," and were called the "Great" or "O" Antiphons (the word
antiphon meaning psalm or anthem). These hymns apparently were
restructured into verse form in the 1100s and finally published in Latin in
1710. In the mid–1800s, they were discovered by an English minister
named John Mason Neale, who wove together segments of them to
produce the first draft of "O Come, O Come Emmanuel," which was
published in 1851. Neale's original version said, "Draw nigh, draw nigh,
Emmanuel."

Neale is a man worth knowing. He was born in London on January
24, 1818, the son of an evangelical Anglican clergyman. He attended
Cambridge University and proved to be a brilliant student and
prize–winning poet. While there, Neale was influenced by the Oxford
Movement and became attracted to Roman Catholicism. In 1841, he was
ordained into the Anglican ministry, but his poor health and Catholic
leanings prevented him from gaining a parish ministry.

He was appointed instead as the director of Sackville College, a home for old men. (Sackville College, started by Robert Sackville, Earl of Dorset, in the early 1600s as a home for the elderly, is still going strong today in East Grinstead, Sussex.) This was the perfect job for Neale, for he was a compassionate man with a great heart for the needy, but he was also a scholar needing time for research and writing.

As a high church traditionalist, Neale disliked the hymns of Isaac Watts and longed to return Christianity to the liturgical dignity of church history. He was an outspoken advocate of returning former church buildings to their former glory. He campaigned, for example, against certain types of ugly heating stoves that spoiled the tastefulness and charm of English churches. He also worked hard to translate ancient Greek and Latin hymns into English.

In today's hymnals, we find Neale and Watts side–by–side, the old differences having been forgotten. We owe a debt of gratitude to John Mason Neale every time we sing one of his Christmas carols: "Good King Wenceslas" (see page 68), "Good Christian Men Rejoice," and his Palm Sunday hymn, "All Glory, Laud, and Honor."

Except the Christ be born again tonight
In dreams of all men, saints and sons of shame,
The world will never see his kingdom bright.

VACHEL LINDSAY

The Word became flesh that He might become
enfleshed in all men, thus crowning the created
universe in the redemption of new–created souls.

F. F. SHANNON

For thus says the High and Lofty One
Who inhabits eternity, whose name is Holy:
"I dwell in the high and holy place,
With him who has a contrite and humble spirit,
To revive the spirit of the humble,
And to revive the heart of the contrite ones . . .
I create the fruit of the lips:
Peace, peace to him who is far off
and to him who is near,"
Says the LORD,
"And I will heal him."

ISAIAH 57:15, 19

Thus we can always know that men could live with
goodwill and understanding for each other,
because one day in each year the little Divine
Prince of Peace still compels them to do it.

CHARLES JEREMIAH WELLS

O Come, O Come, Emmanuel

Latin Hymn, 9th cent.
Translated by John M. Neale

Thomas Helmore

1. O come, O come, Em - man - u - el, And ran-som cap - tive
2. O come, thou Wis - dom from on high, Who or-derest all things
3. O come, De - sire of na - tions, bind All peo-ples in one
4. O come, thou Day-spring, come and cheer Our spir - its by Thine

Is - ra - el, That mourns in lone - ly ex - ile here
might - i - ly; To us the path of knowl - edge show
heart and mind. From dust Thou brought us forth to life;
ad - vent here; Dis - perse the gloom - y clouds of night,

Un - til the Son of God ap - pear.
And teach us in her ways to go.
De - liv - er us from earth - ly strife.
And death's dark shad-ows put to flight.

Re - joice! Re - joice! Em-

man - u - el, Shall come to thee, O Is - ra - el!

Good King Wenceslas
1854

"But when you give a feast, invite the poor, the
maimed, the lame, the blind. And you will be
blessed, because they cannot repay you; for you
shall be repaid at the resurrection of the just."

LUKE 14:13–14

This story is about two men—a Bohemian Duke and an Anglican
minister—who lived nearly a thousand years apart.

Wenceslas was born in Bohemia, in modern Czechoslovakia, in the
early 900s. His father, the Czech ruler Duke Ratislav, gave him a good
education supervised by his godly grandmother. When his father died,
Wenceslas, seeing his mother mishandle affairs of state, stepped in to
seize the reins of government at age 18. From the beginning, he proved a
different sort of king. He sought good relations with surrounding
nations, particularly with Germany. He took steps to reform the judicial
system, reducing the number of death sentences and the arbitrary power
of judges. He encouraged the building of churches and showed heartfelt
concern for the poor. He reportedly cut firewood for orphans and widows,
often carrying the provisions on his own shoulders through the snow.

Wenceslas' brief reign ended suddenly. His pagan and rebellious
brother, Boleslav, murdered him on September 28, 929, as he left for
church. His people venerated him as a martyr, and today Wenceslas is the
patron saint of Czechoslovakia.

He would hardly be remembered, however, but for John Mason Neale, a minister with a passion for returning church architecture and music to their ancient grandeur. Neale helped establish a committee to investigate and restore dilapidated church buildings in Great Britain.

Disliking the hymns of Isaac Watts, he also sought to return church music to its medieval roots. Neale worked hard to translate ancient Greek, Latin, and Syrian hymns into English. In so doing, he gave us the Christmas carols, "Good Christian Men Rejoice" (a fourteenth–century text set to a fourteenth–century tune) and "O Come, O Come Emmanuel" (a ninth–century text set to a fifteenth–century tune, see page 64). He also translated the Palm Sunday hymn "All Glory, Laud, and Honor."

"Good King Wenceslas" is not a translation, but an original poem written by Neale to honor a godly monarch's concern for the poor. Neale himself worked with the needy, serving as warden of a charitable residence for indigent old men.

John Neale's antiquated opinions were widely scorned in his own time, but today we're still singing his songs.

Christmas! 'Tis the season for kindling
the fire of hospitality in the hall, the
genial fire of charity in the heart.

WASHINGTON IRVING

Command those who are rich in this present age
not to be haughty, nor to trust in uncertain riches
but in the living God, who gives us richly all things
to enjoy. Let them do good, that they be rich in
good works, ready to give, willing to share, storing
up for themselves a good foundation for the time
to come, that they may lay hold on eternal life.

1 Timothy 6:17–19

Christmas, my child, is love in action. . . .
When you love someone, you give to them,
as God gives to us. The greatest gift He ever
gave was the Person of His Son, sent to us
in human form so that we might know what
God the Father is really like! Every time
we love, every time we give, it's Christmas.

Dale Evans Rogers

Jesus called them to Himself and said to them . . .
"Whoever desires to become great among you shall
be your servant. And whoever of you desires to be
first shall be slave of all. For even the Son of Man
did not come to be served, but to serve, and to give
His life a ransom for many."

Mark 10:42–45

Good King Wenceslas

John M. Neale

Swedish Carol

1. Good King Wen-ces-las looked out on the Feast of Ste-phen,
2. "Hith-er, page, and stand by me, if you know it, tell-ing,
3. "Bring me food and bring me wine, bring me pine logs hith-er,
4. "Sire, the night is dark-er now, and the wind blows stron-ger,
5. In his mas-ter's steps he trod, where the snow lay dint-ed;

When the snow lay round a-bout, deep and crisp and e-ven.
Yon-der peas-ant, who is he? Where and what his dwell-ing?"
You and I will see him dine, when we bear them thith-er."
Fails my heart, I know not how; I can go no long-er."
Heat was in the ver-y sod which the saint had print-ed.

Bright-ly shone the moon that night, though the frost was cru-el,
"Sire, he lives a good league hence, un-der-neath the moun-tain,
Page and mon-arch, forth they went, forth they went to-geth-er,
"Mark my foot-steps, my good page, tread now in them bold-ly,
There-fore, Chris-tian men, be sure, wealth or rank pos-sess-ing,

When a poor man came in sight, gath-ering win-ter fu-el.
Right a-gainst the for-est fence, by Saint Ag-nes' foun-tain."
Through the cold wind's wild la-ment and the bit-ter weath-er.
You shall find the win-ter's rage freeze your blood less cold-ly."
You who now will bless the poor shall your-selves find bless-ing.

Now Praise We Christ the Holy One
1854

Let them praise the name of the LORD,
For His name alone is exalted;
His glory is above the earth and heaven.

Beneath the merriment of Christmas, a melancholy stream flows like an underground river. It isn't simply feelings of nostalgia or the holiday blues; it's the pathos of the imponderable—the unsearchable sorrow of God–in–flesh coming to die for the sins of the world.

If we miss this feeling, somehow we've missed Christmas.

I think the very oldest hymns of Christmas best open our hearts to these bittersweet feelings of wonder. Few experiences are more powerful, for example, than attending a Christmas Eve worship service and hearing the somber strains of the ancient canticle "Now Praise We Christ the Holy One."

Hearing it, one has the sense of attending midnight Mass in an ancient torch–lit cathedral on Christmas Eve, or being present in the halls of a medieval monastery as brown–robed monks shuffle through the cloisters, their haunting chants echoing through the shadowed corridors. Consider how this simple verse cuts to the heart of the mysterious wonder of Christmas:

Upon a manger filled with hay / In poverty content He lay;
With milk was fed the Lord of all, / Who feeds the ravens when they call.

Caelius Sedulius was a Latin Christian who lived in the 400s, probably in Rome. We know little about him except that he seems to have been an expert in pagan literature who, following his conversion, devoted himself to writing Christian poetry and became one of the most influential hymnists in the early church.

"Now Praise We Christ," originally part of a longer Latin hymn entitled *A Solis Ortus Cardine*, was excerpted and translated into German by Martin Luther in the 1520s and rendered into English in 1854 by Richard Massie, an Anglican rector in Eccleston, England.

We don't want to live in dark moods of imponderable mystery, but neither do we want to miss them altogether. They allow us to emerge from the tender sadness of the manger to sing with the angels in the skies above the shepherds' field, even as Sedulius wrote in another ancient carol lifted from *A Solis Ortus Cardine*:

> *From east to west, from shore to shore,*
> *Let every heart awake and sing*
> *The holy child whom Mary bore,*
> *The Christ, the everlasting King.*

"Glory" saints and angels sang: heaven with their praises rang; while shepherds saw with wondering eyes the shepherd who had made the world.

SEDULIUS

And suddenly a voice came from
heaven, saying, "This is My beloved
Son, in whom I am well pleased."

MATTHEW 3:17

This is the irrational season
When love blooms bright and wild.
Had Mary been filled with reason
There'd have been no room for the Child.

MADELEINE L'ENGLE

Therefore, having been justified by faith,
we have peace with God through our
Lord Jesus Christ, through whom also we
have access by faith into this grace in which we
stand, and rejoice in hope of the glory of God.

ROMANS 5:1–2

Now Praise We Christ the Holy One

Caelius Sedulius   from *Eyn Enchyridion*

1. Now praise we Christ, the Ho - ly One,
2. He Who Him - self all things did make
3. The no - ble moth - er bore a Son—
4. Up - on a man - ger filled with hay
5. The heav - enly choirs re - joice and raise

The bless - ed vir - gin Mar - y's Son,
A ser - vant's form vouch - safed to take
For so did Ga - briel's prom - ise run—
In pov - er - ty con - tent He lay;
Their voice to God in songs of praise.

Far as the glo - rious sun doth shine,
That He as man man - kind might win
Whom John con - fessed and leaped with joy
With milk was fed the Lord of all,
To hum - ble shep - herds is pro - claimed

1.2.3.4.

5.

E'en to the world's re - mote con - fine.
And save His crea - tures from their sin.
Ere yet the moth - er knew her Boy.
Who feeds the rav - ens when they call.
The Shep - herd Who the world hath framed.

Of the Father's Love Begotten
1854

"For God so loved the world that He gave His
only begotten Son, that whoever believes in Him
should not perish but have everlasting life."

JOHN 3:16

Last year a college student sauntered into my office to tell me about a new
song he'd discovered, one with haunting melody and pensive words, and
pulling out a CD, he played it for me. I smiled when I realized his "new"
song was one of our oldest hymns, "Of the Father's Love Begotten."

This ancient Latin hymn is by Aurilius Clemens Prudentius, who was
born in northern Spain in AD 348, not long after Christianity was
legalized in the Roman Empire following three centuries of persecution.
Prudentius became a lawyer and provincial governor in Spain, where his
leadership skills attracted the attention of Emperor Theodosius I. He was
then appointed to an imperial military post.

It may have been shortly afterward that Prudentius gave his life to
Christ and began writing Christian poetry. At age fifty–seven, he retired
from government service and entered a monastery where he devoted
himself exclusively to worship and writing. Today we have nearly
four hundred poems from his hand. His *Psychomachia* ("The Contest of
the Soul") was the first completely allegorical poem in European
literature and cast a long shadow over medieval times.

Prudentius has been called "the prince of early Christian poets."
Although he and Ambrose ("Come, Thou Redeemer of the Earth",

see page 84) both were writing hymns about the same time, the ones by Prudentius are more reflective, displaying greater warmth and glow. Perhaps it was his warm Spanish blood.

"Of the Father's Love Begotten" is among the greatest Christmas carols in western history, and thankfully its popularity is on the increase, partly owing to the tender beauty of its probing score, DIVINUM MYSTERIUM, composed nearly a thousand years ago. John Mason Neale translated the poem from Latin into English in 1854.

My young collegian would say that if you've never heard "Of the Father's Love Begotten," throw down this book and run—don't walk—to your nearest music store and find a quality recording of it. I agree. It's worth learning.

Of the Father's love begotten, ere the worlds began to be,
He is Alpha and Omega, He the source, the ending He,
Of the things that are, that have been, and that future years shall see,
Evermore and evermore!
O that birth for ever blessed! When the virgin, full of grace,
By the Holy Ghost conceiving, bare the Savior of our race,
And the babe, the world's redeemer, first revealed his sacred face,
Evermore and evermore!

Jesus Christ, the condescension of
divinity, and the exaltation of humanity.

PHILLIPS BROOKS

In this the love of God was manifested toward
us, that God has sent His only begotten Son
into the world, that we might live through Him.

1 John 4:9

We are celebrating the feast of the Eternal
Birth which God the Father has borne and
never ceases to bear in all eternity . . . But if it
takes not place in me, what avails it? Everything
lies in this, that it should take place in me.

Meister Eckhart

"Believe Me that I am in the Father and
the Father in Me, or else believe Me
for the sake of the works themselves."

John 14:11

Of the Father's Love Begotten

Aurelius Prudentius   Sanctus Trope, 11th century

1. Of the Fa - ther's love be - got - ten,
2. At His Word the worlds were fram - èd;
3. O ye heights of heav'n a - dore Him;
4. Christ, to Thee with God the Fa - ther,

ere the worlds be - gan to be, He is Al - pha and O - me - ga,
He com - mand - ed; it was done: Heav'n and earth and depths of o - cean
an - gel hosts, His prais - es sing; Powers, do - min - ions, bow be - fore Him,
and, O Ho - ly Ghost, to Thee, Hymn and chant with high thanks-giv - ing,

He the source, the End - ing He, Of the things that are, that have been,
in their three - fold or - der one; All that grows be - neath the shin - ing
and ex - tol our God and King! Let no tongue on earth be si - lent,
and un - wea - ried prais - es be: Hon - or, glo - ry, and do - min - ion,

And that fu - ture years shall see, ev - er - more and ev - er - more!
Of the moon and burn - ing sun, ev - er - more and ev - er - more!
Ev - ery voice in con - cert sing, ev - er - more and ev - er - more!
And e - ter - nal vic - to - ry, ev - er - more and ev - er - more!

We Three Kings of Orient Are
1857

Now after Jesus was born in Bethlehem of
Judea in the days of Herod the king, behold,
wise men from the East came to Jerusalem.

MATTHEW 2:1

Strange but true: A visit from St. Nicholas paved the way for "We
Three Kings." It happened like this. After the War of 1812, Anglicans
in America decided to establish their own seminary for training
Episcopalian ministers. The proposal was first made in 1814, and in 1817
the Episcopalian General Convention voted to locate the school in New
York City. But where in New York?

Clement Clarke Moore, son of New York's Episcopalian Bishop, was
an up–and–coming land developer. He had recently become well–known
because of a poem he had written, which began:

'Twas the night before Christmas, when all through the house

not a creature was stirring, not even a mouse . . .

The popularity of the poem (reportedly written following a sleigh
ride home from Greenwich Village) made his name a household word.
The fame and increased income made him a more generous and
sought–after layman.

Moore owned a large estate in the undeveloped northern regions of
Manhattan. He referred to it as "a quiet, rural retreat on the picturesque
banks of the Hudson." Hearing that the Episcopalians needed land for

their seminary, he offered a portion of his estate, and thus was born General Theological Seminary. Moore, also a linguist and Hebrew scholar, became one of General's first professors, teaching biblical languages.

Some years later, a reporter named John H. Hopkins, Jr., enrolled in this seminary. Born in Pittsburg, Hopkins had matriculated at the University of Vermont before moving to New York to pursue legal studies. But he fell in love with the Lord's work, enrolled in General, and graduated from the seminary in 1850. In 1855, he was hired as the school's first instructor of church music.

Hopkins wrote "We Three Kings" as part of a Christmas pageant produced by General Theological Seminary in 1857. In 1863 it was published in his *Carols, Hymns, and Songs*. This hymnal went through three editions by 1882, establishing Hopkins as a leader in Episcopalian hymnody. He wrote other hymns, but most have fallen into obscurity. "We Three Kings" was his crowning achievement, made possible, in a way, through the generosity of another poet whose most famous work ends:

> *But I heard him exclaim, 'ere he drove out of sight,*
> *Merry Christmas to all, and to all a good night!*

"What means this glory round our feet,"
The Magi mused, "more bright than morn!"
And voices chanted clear and sweet,
"To–day the Prince of Peace is born."

JAMES RUSSELL LOWELL

Christmas gift suggestions: To your enemy,
forgiveness. To an opponent, tolerance. To a
friend, your heart. To a customer, service. To all,
charity. To every child, a good example. To
yourself, respect.

OREN ARNOLD

When they heard the king, they departed;
and behold, the star which they had seen
in the East went before them, till it came
and stood over where the young Child was.
When they saw the star, they rejoiced
with exceedingly great joy.

MATTHEW 2:9–10

That was the true Light which gives light
to every man coming into the world.

JOHN 1:9

We Three Kings of Orient Are

John H. Hopkins, Jr.   John H. Hopkins, Jr.

1. We three kings of O - ri - ent are, Bear-ing gifts we trav - erse a - far;
2. Born a King on Beth-le-hem's plain, Gold I bring to crown Him a - gain;
3. Frank-in - cense to of - fer have I, In-cense owns a De - i - ty nigh;
4. Myrrh is mine, its bit - ter per - fume, Breathes a life of gath - er-ing gloom;
5. Glo - rious now be - hold Him a - rise, King and God and Sac - ri - fice;

Field and foun - tain, moor and moun - tain, Fol - low-ing yon - der star.
King for - ev - er, ceas - ing nev - er, O - ver us all to reign.
Prayer and prais - ing, all men rais - ing, Wor-ship Him, God on high.
Sor - rowing, sigh-ing, bleed-ing, dy - ing, Sealed in the stone cold tomb.
Al - le - lu - ia, al - le - lu - ia! Earth to heav'n re - plies.

O star of won-der, star of night, Star with roy-al beau-ty bright;

West-ward lead-ing, still pro - ceed-ing, Guide us to Thy per - fect light.

Come, Thou Redeemer of the Earth

1862

I know that my Redeemer lives,
And He shall stand at last on the earth.

This carol stretches back into the early, misty centuries of Christian history. It was written by the mighty Ambrose, bishop of Milan, whose personal story is as remarkable as his carol is wonderful.

Ambrose was born about AD 340 in Gaul (modern France), where his father was governor before moving his family to Rome. In the empire's capital Ambrose became a noted poet, a skilled orator, and a respected lawyer. At age thirty–four, he was named governor of an Italian province and headquartered in Milan.

A crisis arose in Milan after the death of popular Bishop Auxentius as the city argued about his replacement. Tensions ran high. Assembling the people, Ambrose used his oratorical powers to appeal for unity; but while he was speaking, a child reportedly cried out: "Let Ambrose be bishop!" The crowd took up the chant, and the young governor, to his dismay, was elected the city's pastor.

Taking the call seriously, Ambrose became a great preacher and a deft defender of true doctrine. He wrote books and treatises, sermons, hymns, and letters. He tended Milan like a shepherd. Under his preaching a young, hot–blooded infidel named Aurelius Augustine was converted to Christ, and St. Augustine went on to become one of the greatest heroes in the history of Christian theology.

Ambrose continued preaching until he fell sick in AD 397. When distressed friends prayed for his healing, he replied, "I have so lived among you that I cannot be ashamed to live longer, but neither do I fear to die; for we have a good Lord." On Good Friday, April 3, Ambrose lay with his hands extended in the form of the cross, moving his lips in prayer. His friends huddled in sadness and watched. Sometime past midnight, their beloved bishop passed to his good Lord.

Sixteen centuries have come and gone, and today the hymns of Ambrose are better known than his sermons. His beloved Christmas carol, *Veni, Redemptor gentium*, was translated from Latin by John Mason Neale in 1862 and set to a lovely, lilting fifteenth century melody named Puer Nobis Nascitur.

"The Redeemer will come to Zion,
And to those who turn from transgression in
Jacob," Says the Lord. "As for Me," says the Lord,
"this is My covenant with them: My Spirit who is
upon you, and My words which I have put in your
mouth, shall not depart from your mouth, nor
from the mouth of your descendants, nor from the
mouth of your descendants' descendants," says
the Lord, "from this time and forevermore."

Isaiah 59:20–23

Born of the Virgin, He came forth from the womb
as the light of the whole world to shine on all. His
light is received by those who long for the splendor
of perpetual light that can never be destroyed by
darkness. The sun we know every day is followed
by the darkness of night, but the sun of righteousness
never sets, because wisdom cannot give way to evil.

AMBROSE

Sing, O heavens, for the LORD has done it!
Shout, you lower parts of the earth;
Break forth into singing, you mountains,
O forest, and every tree in it!
For the LORD has redeemed Jacob,
And glorified Himself in Israel.

ISAIAH 44:23

When we speak about wisdom, we are speaking of Christ.
When we speak about virtue, we are speaking of Christ.
When we speak about justice, we are speaking of Christ.
When we speak about peace, we are speaking of Christ.
When we speak about truth and life and redemption,
we are speaking of Christ.

AMBROSE

Come, Thou Redeemer of the Earth

Ambrose of Milan
Trans. by John M. Neale

15th century
Adapted by Michael Praetorius

1. Come, Thou Re - deem - er of the earth,
2. Be - got - ten of no hu - man will,
3. The vir - gin womb that bur - den gained
4. Thy cra - dle here shall glit - ter bright,

And man - i - fest Thy vir - gin birth:
But of the Spir - it, Thou art still
With vir - gin hon - or all un - stained;
And dark - ness breathe a new - er light,

Let ev - ery age a - dor - ing fall;
The Word of God in flesh ar - rayed,
The ban - ners there of vir - tue glow;
Where end - less faith shall shine se - rene,

Such birth be - fits the God of all.
The prom - ised Fruit to man dis - played.
God in His tem - ple dwells be - low.
And twi - light nev - er in - ter - vene.

Angels We Have Heard on High
1862

And suddenly there was with the angel a
multitude of the heavenly host praising
God and saying: "Glory to God in the highest,
And on earth peace, goodwill toward men!"

LUKE 2:13–14

"Les Anges dans nos Campagnes" was a French carol dating from the 1700s, which appeared in several different versions. It was published in English in 1862 with the words familiar to us today.

But an older version had the title "Harken All! What Holy Singing!" The words, translated into English, said:

> *Hearken, all! What holy singing*
> *Now is sounding from the sky!*
> *'Tis a hymn with grandeur ringing,*
> *Sung by voices clear and high.*
> *Gloria, in excelsis Deo!*

Still another primitive version speaks from the shepherds' vantage point, saying:

> *Shepherds in the field abiding,*
> *Tell us when the seraph bright*
> *Greeted you with wondrous tiding,*

What you saw and heard that night.
Gloria, in excelsis Deo!

Hymns usually are authored by human beings like us, but in this case obscure verses by unknown French poets were coupled with a refrain that literally was composed by angels in heaven: *Gloria, in excelsis Deo*. That's the Latin wording for the angelic anthem, "Glory to God in the highest!" It comes from Luke 2:14 in the Vulgate, the Latin version of the Bible. The Latin word *Gloria* means "Glory," and *in excelsis* is the phrase for "in the highest." Our English words *excel* and *excellent* come from the same root, meaning "to rise" or "to be high." The Latin word *Deo* means "God."

This was the song proclaimed by the angels over Shepherds' Field the night Christ was born. The musical score emphasizes the words in a way that is uniquely fun to sing and deeply stirring, as we lift our voices to proclaim: A Savior is born! *Gloria, in excelsis Deo!*

Oh! lovely voices of the sky
Which hymned the Saviour's birth.

FELICIA HEMANS

Then the Angel of the LORD . . . said,
"I will never break My covenant with you."

JUDGES 2:1

God sent his Singers upon earth
With songs of sadness and of mirth,
That they might touch the hearts of men,
And bring them back to heaven again.

HENRY WADSWORTH LONGFELLOW

Give unto the LORD, O you mighty ones,
Give unto the LORD glory and strength.
Give unto the LORD the glory due to His name;
Worship the LORD in the beauty of holiness . . .
The LORD will give strength to His people;
The LORD will bless His people with peace.

PSALM 29:1–2, 11

Angels We Have Heard on High

French Carol   French Melody

1. An - gels we have heard on high   Sweet - ly sing - ing o'er the plains,
2. Shep - herds, why this ju - bi - lee?   Why your joy - ous strains pro - long?
3. Come to Beth - le - hem and see   Him whose birth the an - gels sing;

And the moun - tains in re - ply   Ech - o - ing their joy - ous strains.
What the glad - some tid - ings be,   Which in - spire your heav'n - ly song?
Come a - dore on bend - ed knee,   Christ the Lord, the new - born King.

Glo - - - - - - - - - ri - a

in ex - cel - sis De - o! Glo - - - - - -

ri - a in ex - cel - sis De - o!

Thou Didst Leave Thy Throne
1864

Let this mind be in you which was also in Christ
Jesus, who, being in the form of God, did not
consider it robbery to be equal with God, but
made Himself of no reputation, taking the form of
a bondservant, and coming in the likeness of men.

PHILIPPIANS 2:5–7

Emily Elliott was born south of London in the little holiday town of Brighton on the English Channel in 1836. Her father, Edward Elliott, was pastor of St. Mark's Church there. His invalid aunt—Charlotte Elliott, well-known hymnist and the author of the invitational hymn "Just As I Am"—lived nearby.

While working with children in the church choir and the local parish school, Emily, in her late twenties, wanted to use the Christmas season to teach them about the entire life and mission of the Savior. As she studied Luke 2:7, she wrote this hymn. The first and second verses speak of our Lord's birth, but the third verse describes His life as an itinerate preacher. The next stanza describes His death on Calvary, and the last verse proclaims His Second Coming.

Emily had her hymn privately printed, and it was first performed in her father's church during the Christmas season of 1864. Six years later, she included it in a magazine she edited called *Church Missionary Juvenile Instructor.*

Several years later, Emily inserted this carol into her book of poems and hymns entitled *Chimes for Daily Service*. "Thou Didst Leave Thy Throne" first appeared in the United States in *The Sunday School Hymnal*, published in Boston in 1871.

Emily devoted her life to Sunday school work, to ministering to the down–and–out in Brighton's rescue missions, and to sharing the message of Christ through poems, hymns, and the printed page. Another of her carols was widely used for many years during the Christmas season, although it isn't well–known today. The words are ideally suited for the children Emily so loved. This carol, too, encompasses our Lord's entire life and mission:

There came a little Child to earth long ago;
And the angels of God proclaimed His birth, high and low.
Out on the night, so calm and still, their song was heard;
For they knew that the Child on Bethlehem's hill was Christ the Lord.
In mortal weakness, want and pain, He came to die,
That the children of earth might in glory reign with Him on high.
And evermore in robes so fair and undefiled,
Those ransomed children His praise declare, who was a Child.

He became what we are that
He might make us what He is.

———

ATHANASIUS

Thus says the LORD:
"Heaven is My throne, And earth is My footstool.
Where is the house that you will build Me?
And where is the place of My rest?
For all those things My hand has made,
And all those things exist,"
Says the Lord. "But on this one will I look:
On him who is poor and of a contrite spirit,
And who trembles at My word."

ISAIAH 66:1–2

His descent to our lowliness is
the supreme expression of his power.

GREGORY OF NYSSA

The heavens are Yours, the earth also is Yours;
The world and all its fullness, You have founded them. . . .
Righteousness and justice are the foundation of Your throne;
Mercy and truth go before Your face.
Blessed are the people who know the joyful sound!
They walk, O LORD, in the light of Your countenance.

PSALM 89:11, 14–15

Thou Didst Leave Thy Throne

Emily E. S. Elliott

Timothy R. Matthews

1. Thou didst leave Thy throne and Thy king - ly crown When Thou
2. Heav - en's arch - es rang when the an - gels sang, Pro -
3. The fox - es found rest, and the birds their nest In the
4. Thou cam - est, O Lord, with the liv - ing word That should
5. When the heavens shall ring and the an - gels sing At Thy

cam - est to earth for me, But in Beth - le - hem's home was there
claim - ing Thy roy - al de - cree, But of low - ly birth didst Thou
shade of the for - est tree; But Thy couch was the sod, O Thou
set Thy peo - ple free; But with mock - ing scorn and with
com - ing to vic - tor - y, Let Thy voice call me home, say - ing,

found no room For Thy ho - ly na - tiv - i - ty. O come to my
come to earth And in great hu - mil - i - ty. O come to my
Son of God, In the des - erts of Gal - i - lee. O come to my
crown of thorn They bore Thee to Cal - va - ry. O come to my
"Yet there is room, There is room at My side for thee." And my heart shall re -

heart, Lord Je - sus: There is room in my heart for Thee!
heart, Lord Je - sus. There is room in my heart for Thee!
heart, Lord Je - sus. There is room in my heart for Thee!
heart, Lord Je - sus. There is room in my heart for Thee!
joice, Lord Je - sus, When Thou com - est and call - est me.

I Heard the Bells on Christmas Day
1864

Behold, He who keeps Israel
Shall neither slumber nor sleep.

The famous Longfellow brothers were born and raised in Portland, Maine, in the 1800s. Henry Wadsworth was born in 1807, and younger brother Samuel arrived in 1819. Henry became a Harvard professor of literature and one of America's greatest writers, and Samuel became a Unitarian minister and a hymnist.

While Henry was publishing his books, however, dark clouds were gathering over his life and over all America. In 1861, his wife tragically died when her dress caught fire in their home in Cambridge, Massachusetts. That same year, the Civil War broke out. Two years later, Henry's son, Charley, age seventeen, ran away from home and hopped aboard a train to join President Lincoln's army.

Charley proved a brave and popular soldier. He saw action at the Battle of Chancellorsville in 1863, but in early June he contracted typhoid fever and malaria and was sent home to recover. He missed the Battle of Gettysburg, but by August Charley was well enough to return to the field. On November 27, during the Battle of New Hope Church in Virginia, he was shot through the left shoulder. The bullet nicked his spine and came close to paralyzing him. He was carried into the church and later taken to Washington to recuperate.

Receiving the news on December 1, 1863, Henry immediately left for Washington. He found his son well enough to travel, and they headed back to Cambridge, arriving home on December 8. For weeks Henry sat by his son's bedside, slowly nursing his boy back to health.

On Christmas Day, December 25, 1863, Henry gave vent to his feelings in this plaintive carol that can only be understood against the backdrop of war. Two stanzas now omitted from most hymnals speak of the cannons thundering in the South and of hatred tearing apart "the hearth–stones of a continent." The poet feels like dropping his head in despair, but then he hears the Christmas bells. Their triumphant pealing reminds him that "God is not dead, nor doth He sleep."

The Sunday school children of the Unitarian Church of the Disciples in Boston first sang this carol during that year's Christmas celebration. How wonderful that such a song could emerge from the bloody clouds of the War Between the States.

When Christmas bells are swinging above
the fields of snow, we hear sweet voices
ringing from lands of long ago, and etched on
vacant places are half–forgotten faces of friends
we used to cherish, and loves we used to know.

Ella Wheeler Wilcox

Praise the LORD!
Praise God in His sanctuary;
Praise Him in His mighty firmament!
Praise Him for His mighty acts;
Praise Him according to His excellent greatness!
Praise Him with the sound of the trumpet;
Praise Him with the lute and harp!
Praise Him with the timbrel and dance;
Praise Him with stringed instruments and flutes!
Praise Him with loud cymbals;
Praise Him with clashing cymbals!
Let everything that has breath praise the LORD.
Praise the Lord!

PSALM 150

Then David and all Israel played music before God
with all their might, with singing, on harps, on
stringed instruments, on tambourines, on
cymbals, and with trumpets.

1 CHRONICLES 13:8

I Heard the Bells on Christmas Day

Henry Wadsworth Longfellow

Jean Baptiste Calkin

1. I heard the bells on Christ - mas day Their
2. And thought how, as the day had come, The
3. And in de - spair I bowed my head: "There
4. Then pealed the bells more loud and deep: "God
5. Till ring - ing, sing - ing on its way, The

old fa - mil - iar car - ols play, And wild and sweet the
bel - fries of all Chris - ten - dom Had rolled a - long th'un -
is no peace on earth," I said, "For hate is strong, and
is not dead, nor doth He sleep; The wrong shall fail, the
world re - volved from night to day, A voice, a chime, a

words re - peat, Of peace on earth, good - will to men.
bro - ken song Of peace on earth, good - will to men.
mocks the song Of peace on earth, good - will to men."
right pre - vail, With peace on earth, good - will to men."
chant sub - lime, Of peace on earth, good - will to men!

What Child Is This?

1865

So it was, when the angels had gone away from
them into heaven, that the shepherds said to one
another, "Let us now go to Bethlehem . . ."

LUKE 2:15

Feelings of sadness come over me whenever I hear this deeply moving carol. It is, after all, set in the key of E minor, the "saddest of all keys." Yet triumphant joy dispels the sadness as we exclaim: "This, this is Christ the King, whom shepherds guard and angels sing."

The melancholic melody is a famous old British tune called GREENSLEEVES, originally a ballad about a man pining for his lost love, the fair Lady Greensleeves. Tradition said it was composed by King Henry VIII for Anne Boleyn. That's unlikely, but we do know that Henry's daughter, Queen Elizabeth I, danced to the tune. Shakespeare referred to it twice in his play *The Merry Wives of Windsor*.

It was licensed to two different printers in 1580, and soon thereafter it was being used with religious texts. Its first association with Christmas came in 1642 in a book titled *New Christmas Carols,* in which it was used with the poem "The Old Year Now Away Has Fled." The last verse says:

> *Come, give's more liquor when I doe call,*
> *I'll drive to each one in this hall . . .*
> *And God send us a happy new yeare!*

For 150 years, however, GREENESLEEVES has been most identified with "What Child Is This?" The words of this carol are taken from a longer poem written by an insurance agent named William Chatterton Dix, born in Bristol, England, in 1837. His father was a surgeon who wanted his son to follow in his footsteps. But having no interest in medicine, William left Bristol Grammar School, moved to Glasgow, and sold insurance.

His greatest love was his prose and poetry for Christ. He wrote two devotional books, a book for children, and scores of hymns, two of which remain popular Christmas carols: "What Child Is This?" and "As with Gladness Men of Old."

All of Dix's hymns should be more widely sung today, for they are masterpieces of poetry, filled with rich spiritual truth. Here's the way he begins his exultant hymn "Alleluia!"

> *Alleluia! Sing to Jesus! His the scepter, his the throne.*
> *Alleluia! His the triumph, His the victory alone.*

Christ is born so that by His birth He might
restore our nature. He became a child, was fed and
grew so that He might bring in the one perfect age
to remain forever as He created it. He holds
mankind up so that they may no longer fall. The
creature He formed of earth He now makes heavenly.

PETER CHRYSOLOGUS

Mary's "yes" is a free, responsible yes by which she accepts becoming the vessel of the new creation to be embodied by her Son, Jesus. It is not the yes of self–denial, almost of irresponsibility, as it has been traditionally presented to us. Mary knows to whom she is committing herself.

ANA MARIA BIDEGAIN

And without controversy great
is the mystery of godliness:
God was manifested in the flesh,
Justified in the Spirit,
Seen by angels,
Preached among the Gentiles,
Believed on in the world,
Received up in glory.

1 TIMOTHY 3:16

Then Simeon blessed them, and said to Mary His mother, "Behold, this Child is destined for the fall and rising of many in Israel, and for a sign which will be spoken against (yes, a sword will pierce through your own soul also), that the thoughts of many hearts may be revealed."

LUKE 2:34–25

What Child Is This?

William C. Dix

English Melody

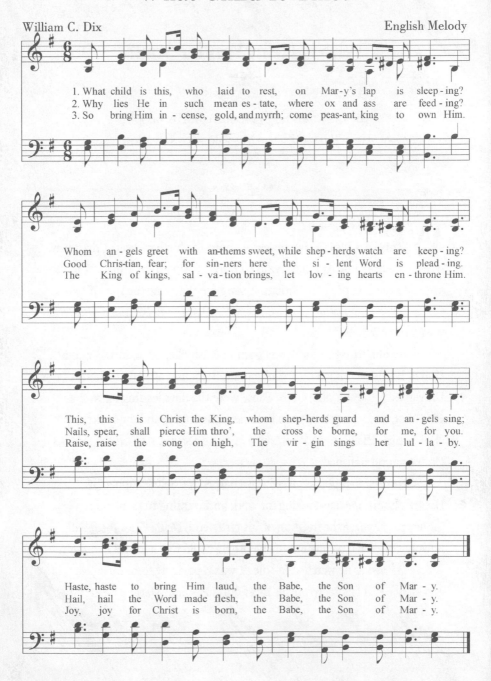

1. What child is this, who laid to rest, on Mar-y's lap is sleep-ing?
2. Why lies He in such mean es - tate, where ox and ass are feed-ing?
3. So bring Him in - cense, gold, and myrrh; come peas-ant, king to own Him.

Whom an - gels greet with an-thems sweet, while shep - herds watch are keep-ing?
Good Chris-tian, fear; for sin-ners here the si - lent Word is plead-ing.
The King of kings, sal - va-tion brings, let lov - ing hearts en - throne Him.

This, this is Christ the King, whom shep-herds guard and an - gels sing;
Nails, spear, shall pierce Him thro', the cross be borne, for me, for you.
Raise, raise the song on high, The vir - gin sings her lul - la - by.

Haste, haste to bring Him laud, the Babe, the Son of Mar - y.
Hail, hail the Word made flesh, the Babe, the Son of Mar - y.
Joy, joy for Christ is born, the Babe, the Son of Mar - y.

Who is He in Yonder Stall?

1866

For the LORD takes pleasure in His people;
He will beautify the humble with salvation.

PSALM 149:4

Would you believe it?

This beautiful Christmas carol about the birth of Jesus Christ was written by the same American who composed "Up on the House Top," arguably the first popular Christmas song emphasizing the role of Santa Claus: *Up on the housetop, click, click, click, / Down thru' the chimney with good Saint Nick.*

Benjamin Russell Hanby was born in Rushville, Ohio, in 1833, to a United Brethren minister. As young man, Benjamin attended Oberlin University in Westerville, Ohio. These were the days leading up to the Civil War, and young Benjamin became a passionate and outspoken abolitionist. His home in Westerville became a secret stop on the famous Underground Railroad.

According to reports, a freed slave named Joe Selby stopped at Hanby's home one day, looking for work and wanting to earn enough money to purchase the freedom of his girlfriend, Nellie Gray. Joe fell ill, however, and died of pneumonia before he could free her, and Benjamin deeply grieved as he watched Joe die. It was reportedly from this experience that Hanby wrote his most famous song, "Darling Nellie Gray."

Oh, my poor Nellie Gray, they have taken you away,
And I'll never see my darling, anymore.
I'm sitting by the river and a'weeping all the day,
For you've gone from the old Kentucky shore.

Hanby sent the song to the Oliver Ditson Company, a Boston publishing firm, but heard nothing back. One day, he learned that "Darling Nellie Gray" was a hit. As it turned out, the executives at Oliver Ditson had filed for the song's copyright in their own names, though still listing him as the author. When he wrote asking for his share of the profits, the company sent him a dozen copies of the sheet music along with a note saying, "We have the money and you have the fame. That balances the account."

Hanby went on to become a college employee, a school principal, a pastor, and a songwriter before dying in his early thirties just after the conclusion of the Civil War.

"Up on the Housetop" was published in about 1860, and "Who is He in Yonder Stall?" was published in 1866, the year before Hanby's death. Today his home, located a block from Otterbein College, is owned by the Ohio Historical Society and is managed by the Westerville Historical Society in his memory.

The hinge of history is on the
door of a Bethlehem stable.

RALPH W. SOCKMAN

He has shown you, O man, what is good;
And what does the LORD require of you
But to do justly, to love mercy,
And to walk humbly with your God?

MICAH 6:8

This is Christmas: not the tinsel, not
the giving and receiving, not even the
carols, but the humble heart that receives
anew the wondrous gift, the Christ.

FRANK MCKIBBEN

Now the birth of Jesus Christ was as follows:
After His mother Mary was betrothed to
Joseph, before they came together, she was
found with child of the Holy Spirit. . . . An angel
of the Lord appeared to him in a dream, saying,
"Joseph, son of David, do not be afraid to take
to you Mary your wife, for that which is conceived
in her is of the Holy Spirit. And she will bring
forth a Son, and you shall call His name Jesus,
for He will save His people from their sins."

MATTHEW 1:18, 20–21

Who Is He in Yonder Stall?

Benjamin R. Hanby

Benjamin R. Hanby

1. Who is He in yon-der stall, At whose feet the shep-herds fall?
2. Who is He the peo-ple bless For His words of gen-tle-ness?
3. Who is He that stands and weeps At the grave where Laz-arus sleeps?
4. Lo! at mid-night, who is He Prays in dark Geth-sem-a-ne?
5. Who is He that from the grave Comes to heal and help and save?

Who is He in deep dis-tress, Fast-ing in the wil-der-ness?
Who is He to whom they bring All the sick and sor-row-ing?
Who is He the gath-ering throng Greet with loud tri-um-phant song?
Who is He on yon-der tree Dies in grief and ag-o-ny?
Who is He that from His throne Rules through all the world a-lone?

'Tis the Lord! O won-drous stor-ry! 'Tis the Lord! the King of

glo-ry! At His feet we hum-bly fall, Crown Him! crown Him, Lord of all!

O Little Town of Bethlehem

1868

"But you, Bethlehem Ephrathah,
Though you are little among the thousands of Judah,
Yet out of you shall come forth to Me the One
to be Ruler in Israel, Whose goings
are from old, from everlasting."

Micah 5:2

At nearly six feet six, weighing nearly three hundred pounds, Phillips Brooks cast a long shadow. He was a native Bostonian, the ninth generation of distinguished Puritan stock, who entered the Episcopalian ministry and pastored with great power in Philadelphia and Boston. His sermons were topical rather than expositional, and he's been criticized for thinness of doctrine. Nonetheless he's considered one of America's greatest preachers.

While at Philadelphia's Holy Trinity Church, Phillips, 30, journeyed to the Holy Land. On December 24, 1865, traveling by horseback from Jerusalem, he attended a five–hour Christmas Eve service at the Church of the Nativity in Bethlehem. He was deeply moved. "I remember standing in the old church in Bethlehem," he later said, "close to the spot where Jesus was born, when the whole church was ringing hour after hour with splendid hymns of praise to God, how again and again it seemed as if I could hear voices I knew well, telling each other of the *Wonderful Night* of the Savior's birth."

Three years later, as he prepared for the Christmas season of 1867, he wanted to compose an original Christmas hymn for the children to sing during their annual program. Recalling his experience in Bethlehem, Brooks wrote a little hymn of five stanzas and handed the words to his organist, Lewis Rednor, saying, "Lewis, why not write a new tune for my poem. If it is a good one, I will name it ST. LEWIS after you."

Lewis struggled with his assignment, complaining of no inspiration. Finally, on the night before the Christmas program, he awoke with the music ringing in his soul. He jotted down the melody, then went back to sleep. The next day, a group of six Sunday school teachers and thirty-six children sang "O Little Town of Bethlehem."

Brooks was so pleased with the tune that he did indeed name it for his organist, changing the spelling to ST. LOUIS, so as not to embarrass him. The fourth stanza, usually omitted from our hymnbooks, says:

Where children pure and happy pray to the blessed Child,
Where misery cries out to Thee, Son of the mother mild;
Where charity stands watching and faith holds wide the door,
The dark night wakes, the glory breaks, and Christmas comes once more.

The incarnation is the supreme assertion that only
through the highest medium, which is humanity,
can the highest messages be given to mankind.

PHILLIPS BROOKS

The feet of the humblest may walk in the fields
Where the feet of the holiest have trod.
This, this is the marvel to mortals revealed,
When the silvery trumpets of Christmas have pealed,
That mankind are the children of God.

PHILLIPS BROOKS

"The sun shall no longer be your light by day,
Nor for brightness shall the moon give light to you;
But the LORD will be to you an everlasting light,
And your God your glory.
Your sun shall no longer go down,
Nor shall your moon withdraw itself;
For the LORD will be your everlasting light,
And the days of your mourning shall be ended."

ISAIAH 60:19–20

Hope deferred makes the heart sick,
But when the desire comes, it is a tree of life.

PROVERBS 13:12

O Little Town of Bethlehem

Phillips Brooks   Lewis H. Redner

1. O   lit - tle town of Beth - le - hem, How still we   see thee lie;
2. For Christ is born of Ma - ry And gath - ered   all a - bove;
3. How si - lent - ly, how si - lent - ly, The won - drous   gift is giv'n;
4. O,   ho - ly child of Beth - le - hem, De - scend to   us we pray;

A - bove thy deep and dream - less sleep, The   si - lent stars   go   by.
While mor - tals sleep the   an - gels keep Their watch of   won - dering love.
So   God im - parts to hu - man hearts, The bless - ings of   His heaven.
Cast   out our sin and   en - ter   in, Be born in   us   to - day.

Yet   in   thy dark streets shin - eth The ev - er - last - ing   Light;
O,   morn - ing stars to - geth - er Pro - claim the ho - ly   birth;
No   ear may hear His com - ing, But   in this world of   sin;
We   hear the Christ - mas an - gels, The great glad tid - ings   tell;

The   hopes and fears of   all   the years, Are   met in   thee to - night.
And   prais - es sing to   God the King And peace to   men on earth.
Where meek souls will Re - ceive Him still, The   dear Christ en - ters in.
O,   come to   us   a - bide with us, Our Lord, Em - man - u - el.

There's a Song in the Air
1872

Praise to the LORD!
Sing to the LORD a new song,
And His praise in the assembly of saints.

PSALM 149:1

For a long time, Josiah Gilbert Holland was known to his friends as a failure at just about everything he tried. Dropping out of high school, he tried his hand at photography, then calligraphy. When those professions didn't pan out, Josiah, age twenty–one, enrolled in Berkshire Medical College. After graduation, he practiced medicine in Springfield, Massachusetts, for a while before quitting to start a newspaper. The paper folded after six months. At length, he joined the editorial staff of another newspaper, *The Springfield Republican*, and there he finally found his niche in writing.

In 1865, the world was stunned by the tragic assassination of Abraham Lincoln. The next year, it was Josiah Holland who published the first major biography of Lincoln. In it, he presented Lincoln as a "true–hearted Christian" and provided a number of stories to reinforce the point. When Lincoln's law partner, William Herndon, read the book, he refuted it. Lincoln was an "infidel," declared Herndon, and he died as an "unbeliever." To this day, historians argue about Lincoln's religious faith, or lack of it. But the notoriety put Josiah Holland on the literary map of his day.

In 1870, he became a founder and the senior editor of *Scribner's Magazine*. He continued publishing books and was quite prolific. In 1872, he published *The Marble Prophecy and Other Poems*. In it were the four stanzas of "There's a Song in the Air." It was an unusual poem, in that the first four lines of each stanza contained six syllables each, but the fifth and sixth lines were twice as long. Two years later, the poem was set to music in a collection of Sunday school songs, but it didn't achieve widespread popularity.

Several years after Josiah's death in 1881, a Latin professor named Karl Pomeroy Harrington read "There's a Song in the Air." Harrington was an amateur musician who had begun writing melodies as a youngster on the small organ in his childhood home. Harrington later inherited that old Estey organ and moved it to his vacation cottage in North Woodstock, New Hampshire. While spending the summer there in 1904, he sat down at the old instrument, pumping the bellows with the foot pedals, and hammered out the lovely melodic tune to which "There's a Song in the Air" is now widely sung.

Next to theology I give music
the highest place of honor.

MARTIN LUTHER

But I will sing of Your power;
Yes, I will sing aloud of Your mercy in the morning;
For You have been my defense
And refuge in the day of my trouble.
To You, O my Strength, I will sing praises;
For God is my defense,
My God of mercy.

PSALM 59:16–17

When your heart is full
of Christ, you want to sing.

CHARLES HADDON SPURGEON

Rejoice in the LORD, O you righteous!
For praise from the upright is beautiful.
Praise the LORD with the harp;
Make melody to Him with an
instrument of ten strings.
Sing to Him a new song;
Play skillfully with a shout of joy.
For the word of the LORD is right,
And all His work is done in truth.
He loves righteousness and justice;
The earth is full of the goodness of the LORD.

PSALM 33:1–5

There's a Song in the Air

Josiah G. Holland

Karl P. Harrington

1. There's a song in the air! There's a star in the sky!
2. There's a tu - mult of joy O'er the won - der - ful birth,
3. In the light of that star Lie the a - ges im - pearled;
4. We re - joice in the light, And we ech - o the song

There's a moth - er's deep prayer, And a ba - by's low cry!
For a Vir - gin's sweet Boy, Is the Lord of the earth.
And that song from a - far Has swept o - ver the world.
That comes down thro' the night From the heav - en - ly throng.

And the star rains its fire while the beau - ti - ful sing,
Lo, the star rains its fire while the beau - ti - ful sing,
Ev - ery hearth is a - flame, and the beau - ti - ful sing
Ay! we shout to the love - ly E - van - gel they bring,

For the man - ger of Beth - le - hem, cra - dles a King!
For the man - ger of Beth - le - hem cra - dles a King!
In the homes of the na - tions that Je - sus is King!
As we greet in His cra - dle our Sav - ior and King!

Away in a Manger
1887

And she brought forth her firstborn Son, and wrapped
Him in swaddling cloths, and laid Him in a manger,
because there was no room for them in the inn.

LUKE 2:7

T his is commonly known as "Luther's Cradle Hymn." But did the great
German Reformer, Martin Luther, really write the words? Did he sing
them by the cradle of his little son, Hans? This is a great mystery in hymnology.

In 1887, "Away in a Manger" appeared in a little book of songs entitled
Dainty Songs for Little Lads and Lasses, published in Cincinnati by the John
Church Company. The songbook was compiled by James R. Murray. A
notation beneath "Away in a Manger" said: *Luther's Cradle Hymn (Composed
by Martin Luther for his children and still sung by German mothers to their little
ones.)* Only stanzas one and two were given.

"Away in a Manger" quickly became America's favorite children's
carol, the words being sung to forty–one different tunes! Everyone
assumed the poem had been written by Martin Luther.

Then in 1945, Richard Hill published a fascinating article entitled
"Not So Far Away in a Manger" in which he announced he had discovered
the first two stanzas of "Away in a Manger" in an 1885 songbook entitled
Little Children's Book, published by German Lutherans in Pennsylvania. No
authorship was given. Nor could Hill find any appearance of this carol in
German church history or in Luther's works.

After extensive research, Hill concluded: "It seems essential to lay [aside] once for all the legend that Luther wrote a carol for his children, which no one else knew anything about, until it suddenly turned up in English dress 400 years later in Philadelphia. Luther can well afford to spare the honor." But he adds, "Although Luther himself had nothing to do with the carol, the colonies of German Lutherans in Pennsylvania almost certainly did."

So the mystery endures. Who wrote "Away in a Manger"? There were apparently two unknown writers: a German Lutheran in Pennsylvania who wrote the first two stanzas, with another unknown author adding a third verse that first appeared in an 1892 songbook published by Charles H. Gabriel.

Well, who cares? Certainly not the generations of children around the world who have come to love and know the little Jesus through this sweet carol, and who have gone to sleep praying:

> *I love Thee, Lord Jesus; look down from the sky*
> *And stay by my cradle till morning is nigh.*

What babe new born is this that in a manger
cries? Near on her lowly bed his happy mother
lies. Oh, see the air is shaken with white and
heavenly wings—This is the Lord of all the
earth, this is the King of kings.

RICHARD WATSON GILDER

There are some of us . . . who think to ourselves,
"If I had only been there! How quick I would have
been to help the Baby. I would have washed His
linen. How happy I would have been to go with the
shepherds to see the Lord lying in the manger!"
Yes, we would. We say that because we know how
great Christ is, but if we had been there at that
time, we would have done no better than the
people of Bethlehem. . . . Why don't we do
it now? We have Christ in our neighbor.

MARTIN LUTHER

I will both lie down in peace, and sleep;
For You alone, O LORD, make me dwell in safety.

PSALM 4:8

The work of righteousness will be peace,
And the effect of righteousness,
quietness and assurance forever.
My people will dwell in a peaceful habitation,
In secure dwellings, and in quiet resting places,

ISAIAH 32:17–18

Away in a Manger

Anonymous

James R. Murray

1. A - way in a man - ger, no crib for a bed,
2. The cat - tle are low - ing, the ba - by a - wakes,
3. Be near me, Lord Je - sus; I ask Thee to stay

The lit - tle Lord Je - sus laid down His sweet head.
But lit - tle Lord Je - sus, no cry - ing He makes.
Close by me for - ev - er, and love me, I pray.

The stars in the sky look down where He lay,
I love Thee, Lord Je - sus, look down from the sky,
Bless all the dear chil - dren in Thy ten - der care,

The lit - tle Lord Je - sus, a - sleep on the hay.
And stay by my cra - dle till morn - ing is nigh.
And take us to heav - en to live with Thee there.

Go, Tell It on the Mountain
1907

Then the shepherds returned, glorifying
and praising God for all the things that
they had heard and seen, as it was told them.

LUKE 2:20

During the bitter days of slavery, black workers on American plantations solaced themselves with song and created a unique form of American hymnology—the Negro spiritual. It was the Jubilee Singers of Fisk University in Nashville, Tennessee, who took the plantation songs of the slaves to the entire world. One of the last "spirituals" to be uncovered and published was this unique Christmas carol, "Go, Tell It on the Mountain."

How did it come about?

John Wesley Work Jr. was born in Nashville, on or about August 6, 1871. His father was choir director for a Nashville church, and he often wrote his own arrangements. John grew up singing in his dad's choirs, and when he enrolled in Fisk University, he became active in its music program, although his primary subjects were history and Latin. Returning to Fisk to work on his master's degree, John eventually was hired as professor of Latin and Greek. But his greatest love was the preservation and performance of the spiritual.

Many of the spirituals had been published, but "Go, Tell It on the Mountain" was largely unknown even though it had been performed by the Jubilee Singers since 1879. Some of the original stanzas were obscure, because spirituals, by definition, were unwritten songs passed from plantation to plantation and from generation to generation. The chorus, however, was crystal clear and highlighted the theme for the whole:

Go, tell it on the mountain
Jesus Christ is born.

Intrigued by the chorus and the melody, John wrote two new stanzas for this song, and it became his custom before sunrise on Christmas morning to take students caroling from building to building, singing "Go, Tell It on the Mountain." The carol was first published in 1909 in *Folk Songs of the Negro as Sung on the Plantations*.

John Work has been called the first black collector of African–American folk songs, a pursuit continued by his two sons, John Wesley Work II and Frederick J. Work. Both young men served on the faculty of Fisk University, working with the Jubilee Singers and collecting and publishing spirituals and folk music.

"Go, Tell It on the Mountain" is a classic in that genre. To slaves in antebellum America, the birth of a liberating Savior was a message to be heralded from the highest mountains.

It still is, for us all.

The spirit of Christmas fulfills
the greatest hunger of mankind.

LORING A. SCHULER

How beautiful upon the mountains
Are the feet of him who brings good news,
Who proclaims peace,
Who brings glad tidings of good things,
Who proclaims salvation,
Who says to Zion,
"Your God reigns!"

ISAIAH 52:7

Christmas is most truly Christmas
when we celebrate it by giving the
light of love to those who need it most.

RUTH CARTER STAPLETON

However, Jesus did not permit him, but said
to him, "Go home to your friends, and tell
them what great things the Lord has done for
you, and how He has had compassion on you."

MARK 5:19

Go, Tell It on the Mountain

John W. Work Jr.

American Folk Song

Unison

Go, tell it on the moun-tain, O-ver the hills and ev-ery-where;

Go, tell it on the moun-tain, That Je-sus Christ is born!

Fine

Harmony

1. While shep-herds kept their watch-ing O'er si-lent flocks by night, Be-
2. The shep-herds feared and trem-bled When lo! A-bove the earth Rang
3. Down in a low-ly man-ger The hum-ble Christ was born, And

D.C. al Fine

hold through-out the heav-ens There shone a ho-ly light.
out the an-gel cho-rus That hailed our Sav-ior's birth.
brought us God's sal-va-tion That bless-ed Christ-mas morn.

Jesus Christ is Born Today!

2005

> While I live I will praise the LORD; I will sing
> praises to my God while I have my being.

PSALM 146:2

Adolf Hitler rose to power in Germany determined to take over the German church and dictate the nation's religion. He falsely accused many of the clergymen of treason, theft, or sexual malpractice; and priests, nuns, and church leaders were arrested on trumped–up charges. Religious publications were suspended. Hitler encouraged couples to be married by state officials rather than by priests and pastors. In 1935, he outlawed prayer in the schools, and he did all he could to replace Bible–reading with Nazi propaganda.

He had greater difficulty with the holidays, because Germans had faithfully observed Easter and Christmas for centuries. He sought instead to keep the holidays but to reinterpret their meaning. Easter became a celebration heralding the arrival of spring, and Christmas was turned into a totally pagan festival. Carols and nativity plays were banned from the schools in 1938, and even the name *Christmas* was changed to *Yuletide*.

Holy days became holidays, and the sacred was secularized.

Today we're amazed to observe the same thing happening in America as social libertarians, aided by the media and the courts, seem determined to drain Christmas of its religious significance and make it a purely secular, pagan holiday.

Let's do whatever it takes to remind our society that one can't even spell the word "Christmas" without *Christ*. We need to stay focused on Him during the season; to proclaim His birth, life, death, and resurrection; to worship Him; and to follow the example of the shepherds—"When they had seen Him, they made widely known the saying which was told them concerning this Child" (Luke 2:17).

Every generation of Christians needs to write its own songs of Christmas. Here is my modest contribution, a new carol set to an old melody, one usually reserved for Easter when we join voices in Charles Wesley's jubilant anthem, "Christ the Lord is Risen Today." The melody, EASTER HYMN, is perhaps our most triumphant hymn setting, written in the early 1700s by an unknown composer.

Why use it only once a year? We can sing the Allelujahs at Christmas, too!

So remember while December
Brings the only Christmas Day,
In the year let there be Christmas
In the things you do and say;
Wouldn't life be worth the living
Wouldn't dreams be coming true
If we kept the Christmas spirit
All the whole year through?

ANONYMOUS: "THE WHOLE YEAR THROUGH"

That which was from the beginning, which we
have heard, which we have seen with our eyes,
which we have looked upon, and our hands have
handled, concerning the Word of life—the life
was manifested, and we have seen, and bear
witness, and declare to you that eternal life which
was with the Father and was manifested to us—
that which we have seen and heard we declare
to you, that you also may have fellowship with
us; and truly our fellowship is with the Father
and with His Son Jesus Christ. And these things
we write to you that your joy may be full.

1 JOHN 1:1–4

It is Christmas in the heart that
puts Christmas in the air.

W. T. ELLIS

Now then, we are ambassadors for Christ,
as though God were pleading through us:
we implore you on Christ's behalf, be reconciled
to God. For He made Him who knew no sin
to be sin for us, that we might become
the righteousness of God in Him.

2 CORINTHIANS 5:20-21

Jesus Christ is Born Today

Robert J. Morgan

from *Lyra Davidica*

1. Je - sus Christ is born to - day! Al - - - le - lu - ia!
2. Heav - enly choirs an - nounce His birth! Al - - - le - lu - ia!
3. Born to die and rise a - gain! Al - - - le - lu - ia!

See Him in the man - ger lay! Al - - - le - lu - ia!
Shep - herd boys pro - claim His worth! Al - - - le - lu - ia!
Con - quering death and hell and sin! Al - - - le - lu - ia!

Ten - der Babe, yet God Most High. Al - - - le - lu - ia!
Sheep and ox - en gath - er round! Al - - - le - lu - ia!
Now a - bove the clouds He lives! Al - - - le - lu - ia!

Ma - ker of the earth and sea and sky. Al - - - le - lu - ia!
Beth - le - hem's shed is ho - ly ground! Al - - - le - lu - ia!
Ev - er - last - ing love and life He gives! Al - - - le - lu - ia!

Worship the Lord in song with recordings from Green Hill® Music. CDs are available
at fine gift stores everywhere. To locate a store in your area, call us at 800.200.4656.
www.greenhillmusic.com

Continue your odyssey through great Christian hymns in these books:

Then Sings My Soul: 150 of the World's Greatest Hymns
Robert J. Morgan explores the real–life events, the tribulations and the
triumphs, and the fascinating details that led to these classic songs of praise.

Then Sings My Soul, Book 2: 150 of the World's Greatest Hymns
Robert J. Morgan again guides music–lovers through the
emotion, drama, and faith behind beloved hymns.

NELSON REFERENCE & ELECTRONIC
A Division of Thomas Nelson Publishers
Since 1798

www.thomasnelson.com

*Jesus Loves Me This I Know: The Remarkable Story
Behind the World's Greatest Children's Song.*
This little song has a great big story, and now
Robert J. Morgan tells it with unparalleled richness.

Amazing Grace: A Country Salute to Great Gospel Hymns
Country music stars share some of their thoughts on hymns and faith.
The book includes a CD of the platinum–selling album
Amazing Grace, Volume 1.

COUNTRYMAN®
A Division of Thomas Nelson Publishers
Since 1798